LEARNI
TO FORGIVE

BY

JASON CANADY

IVTH MAN

FAYETTEVILLE,
NORTH CAROLINA

Learning To Forgive by Jason Canady
Published by IVTH Man Design
P.O. Box 9718
Fayetteville, N.C. 28311
www.learntoforgive.org

Unless otherwise noted, all Scripture quotations are from the Life Application Study Bible, New International Version, published jointly by Tyndale House Publishers, Inc., and Zondervan Publishing House.
Life Application Study Bible copyright © 1988, 1989, 1990, 1991 by Tyndale House Publishers, Inc.

Scriptures marked NKJV are from the New King James Version Copyright © 1983 by Thomas Nelson, Inc.

Disciple lyrics used by permission.

Cover design by Jason Canady
Interior layout by Keith Owen

Printed in the United States by Morris Publishing
3212 East Highway 30
Kearney, NE 68847
1-800-650-7888

DEDICATION

This book is dedicated to the one that loved me when no one else could find the time. He forgave me when I willingly turned away, yet kept me safely in His arms until I returned to Him. He redeemed me, taught me who I am and how to forgive. He is my friend and great reward - Jesus Christ.

SPECIAL THANKS

Without these people this project was a ship without a sail.

-To my mother and father, Ronald & Nell, who instilled in me the fear of God.

- To Karen, my gift from God. Thank you for all the time you gave me at the computer so I could be alone with God.

- To Vernon & Diana Madrid, Dave & Salvina Rogers, Ronald & Nell Canady, Ronnie Canady, and Robin & Keith McLaurin. For their belief in what God was doing through me, for your encouragement and financial support. You were the first to step forward and you have become the tip of the sword!

-To those who sacrificed their personal time and took on the job of editor. Karen Canady, Salvina Rogers, Ronald Canady, and Vivian Rhone.

- To Gerard Golden for lending his programs so we could get out this word! Thanks, Jerry.

- To all of you who couldn't find the time or effort to fit me into your life: You catapulted me into the arms of God.

- To Keith Owen, for laying out the interior of this wonderful book. Thanks for lending your skills and knowledge to the work of the Lord. May God bless you a hundred fold.

TABLE OF CONTENTS

KNOCKED DOWN

Lord can You help me
I've been knocked down by the words of a friend
Give me the power to forgive
and love my neighbor as myself
You've been through what I've been through
You know the kiss of a friend
You proved to me on the cross
that You loved me as Yourself.

- Disciple
"Knocked Down"
(© By 2000 Evangelical sideshow / ASCAP)

PREFACE

It was a sunny, blue sky, white cloud day in April as I sat on the picnic table that is behind my workplace. The breeze rattled the top of the trees and swooped down to surround me, giving me the first smell of spring. I was just coming off my lunch break and spending time in prayer with God. I could feel His presence around me and suddenly He spoke clearly to my heart. I wrote it down quickly on anything I could find, in this case, on the back of my bookmark. I dated it and stuck it back in the crease of my Bible. Ten words from the Creator of the Universe.

4/30/04
The Word of the Lord to His servant Jason:
"I am sending you out. Tell my people to forgive."
I closed my Bible and headed back into work.

INTRODUCTION

Of all the books in the world, the one that has found its way into your hands right now is a book on forgiveness. It is by no accident this book is in your hands and you need to know there are no coincidences with God. In order to abide in true love and fellowship with God, as well as properly function as a Christian, you will need to learn how to forgive. Forgiveness is a cornerstone of our faith in Christ.

Forgiveness is and always will be a major part of the body of Christ. However, I am amazed most Christians do not have a solid foundation on which to process and understand basic forgiving principles. I set out under the direction and authority of the Holy Spirit to write a practical, everyday use of God's principles on forgiveness. The result has become a blue print for healing and releasing of God's grace and love. This book is aimed directly to the ones that need to learn forgiveness the most, God's people. It is for all God's people and that includes every length of walk, race, religious background and doctrine. I truly believe the end is drawing near and most Christians will be completely caught unaware and be snared in the trap of unforgiveness through their lack of understanding and their procrastination of dealing with their wounds. Do not be ignorant of this very important truth. God does not forgive us if we don't forgive each other! This is why we need another book on forgiveness. Unforgiveness is a major problem in the church body today.

Take Forgiveness Very Seriously Because God Does

Loving each other and forgiving each other are very serious subjects in God's eyes and can play a crucial role in our personal walk with God. Forgiveness applies to everyone.

For some of you it will be learned for the first time and for others it will deal with the things you thought were long behind you. Sometimes, in order to get back on the right road, you have to go back to where you made the wrong turn. You will never fulfill the call of God in your life if you hold hatred and bitter resentment toward your fellow brother or sister. Does the foot hate the hand? Does the ear despise the eye? How can the body of Christ, whom He died for, be poisoned with bitterness from within and continue to be healthy and in union, acting as one? Let me ask you this. Do you think you are far enough along in your walk with Christ that you can't be offended? Do you think you are over the one who caused you harm? Try this demonstration on for size.

Picture the one that hurt you and did you wrong or hurt you the most. Now ask yourself, is it okay for them to be with you by your side forever in heaven? Now, how did that feel? Do you have any resentment or reservation about it in your heart? Does that frighten you? Would you want that? As you can see we have some work to do. Try this next illustration. Do you choose to ignore the one that offended you? Can you trust them or are they out of the picture altogether? One of my goals in life is to be just like Christ and to know Him; however, in order to have a relationship with Christ and to get closer to His character, I must forgive. In order to be like Christ, you must forgive. Forgiving each other still proves to be a big hurdle in this race.

Forgiveness Is a Commandment

Forgiveness is a commandment not a suggestion. Don't be discouraged; be hopeful, for when God commands us to do something, He provides a way for us to do it. Also, He will not ask us to do something He Himself wouldn't do, or hasn't already done Himself; we will talk about this later. Unforgiveness is still a major problem in the body of Christ today and it acts like poison starting at an entry point of offense and spreading, making the entire body sick and disabling its overall effectiveness.

It is God's desire and my heart's desire to see you healed, healthy and whole. To do this we are going to go right to the source. We must be healed so we can help others heal. We are going to touch the wound and let ourselves go to the point of origin--- the offense. Sometimes there is no other way but to go back to where the wrong turn was made. To do this we might have to go back to childhood and face some things we have hid for so long or maybe we need to go back to just this morning. Because being offended or hurt is part of our makeup of being human, we are dealing with an everyday issue of life. Most people are walking around right now with past hurts and wounds. Jesus said in Luke 17:1, "It is impossible that no offenses should come...", which tells us these situations will arise and arise often, it's how you deal with them that makes the difference.

This book is not about the offense; rather it's about how to handle and process the offense. It's all about forgiveness; it's about healing past hurts and how to handle future ones. We're not just going to diagnose the problem and get the healing we need, we are going to identify and learn to process unforgiveness for the future. Within these pages you will learn what God says about forgiveness, what forgiveness is and what it is not. You will learn how to forgive, how to receive forgiveness for yourself and how to be set free from unforgiveness. Christ came to set us free and loose the chains of all who are oppressed and open the prison doors to those who are bound (Isaiah 61). He wants you free and so do I. Are you ready to be set free? Let's get started. Let's pray together before we begin.

Heavenly Father, I come before you in Jesus' name. I thank You for Your forgiveness and Your exceeding, abounding love for me. I ask You to speak to me by the power of Your Holy Spirit while I read this book. I ask You to please reveal to me the area or people in my life I have not forgiven and areas in my life where healing needs to take place. I give You permission to touch those areas of my heart so that You may bring healing to my life. Give me strength and boldness to do and be all I need to be. Thank You for Your healing and forgiveness in Jesus' name. Amen.

PART ONE

EXAMINING OURSELVES
IN THE BRAZEN LAVER

Therefore you are inexcusable, O man,
whoever you are who judge, for whatever you judge another
you condemn yourself; for you who judge, practice the same things.

~ Apostle Paul from Romans 2:1

CHAPTER

1

THE SECRET OF FORGIVENESS

Bear with each other and forgive whatever grievances you may have against one another. Forgive as the Lord forgave you.
Colossians 3:12

No one noticed what time of day it was. It was around 3 o'clock in the afternoon. Traditional sacrifice time. Atonement time. However, this is no ordinary sacrifice, this sacrifice offers the promise of full restoration to God, by God through the death of His own son. The baking desert sun that normally burns hot over Israel's sand is now struggling to keep its intensity as it makes its descent towards the west, setting the table for dusk. Today's sacrifice is not an animal; it's a man, a man that chose to be in the very position of the cursed and condemned to death. The body of what used to be recognizable as a human man yet still alive, hangs there, nailed through his wrist and feet to a wooden crucible, assembled crudely in the shape of a cross - wood, his executors made him carry to this spot for his death far outside the city walls.

He is abandoned by His family, friends and even by

God Himself. His mother and close friends are standing at a distance, powerless to intervene on his behalf. He was blameless and without fault with not even one sin to condemn Him. He was betrayed by those closest to Him, those who ate at his table and called Him friend. His trust was sold for a price and betrayed with a kiss, labeled an enemy of the people and tried in court unjustly. No one came to his defense and He did not defend Himself. Now He hangs on this crucifixion cross as a condemned man guilty of treason against God and man. The weight of His body is constricting the air to His lungs as He fights the battle every human does to stay alive. He gasps for air in small amounts as He tries to push Himself up. Each time He cries out in pain from His open wounds on His back where He was beaten and stripped of flesh by the merciless cat-o-nine-tails. This makes His mockers laugh even more.

The tongue that once spoke peace and healing and even calmed the waves now is dried and stuck to the roof of His mouth. His bones are out of joint where they stretched Him to fit the cross. Earlier the tormentors labeled Him "King" and made Him a make shift crown constructed from thorns long and sharp and jammed it into his head. Blood from the severe head lacerations rolls into his eyes as He drifts in and out of consciousness. Blood and sweat sting His eyes, and through blurred vision, He sees He is completely surrounded by people who point and mock Him, their faces are merciless and gleeful. They laugh and shout out to Him "Save yourself!" and "There is no help in God for you!" He hangs there, stripped naked and shamed openly, displayed for all to gaze upon and see. His captors rip apart his clothes and fight for each piece of that precious keepsake as He hangs there disgraced, ashamed, and humiliated. He carries upon Him all the guilt and sin of mankind. He carries on Him all the disease and sickness mankind has and will ever know. He carries on Him all cancers, tumors and suffering. He takes on every lie ever spoken, every unfaithful marriage, every abortion and murder ever committed. He has become every hurtful word ever spoken, every rape and betrayal mankind bitterly knows.

He carries on Him all those with a broken heart, every child that is physically neglected and abused. He is loneliness, poverty and bitterness and every secret hurt man has privately carried on his own. He dies for love of man, not just for the deserving, but for the undeserving. He suffers and dies also for his captors and tormentors that put Him there, all those that nailed the nails and those that falsely accused Him. Every sense of this man is assaulted as they mercilessly laugh in glee at His pain. He hangs there suffocating and broken in two, feeling God has abandoned Him. Those around Him point their fingers and shake their head in disgust.

Then, when they have done their worst, Jesus, the Son of God, lifts His head to the sky and cries in a loud voice, " Father forgive them for they know not what they do." The silence of the crowd is deafening as the Spirit of

Love Himself moves through the hearts of those that did their worst. Their faces show the unbelief and shock of such a statement, such a love... "Who *is* this?" has to be running through their minds. Just then Jesus seals the sacrifice and atonement for you and me, and announces the end of His father's business and to all mankind. "It is finished!" He bows His head and dies. Thunder rolls across Israel.

You Can't Forgive On Your Own.

When discussing personally with people the need for forgiveness and it's commandment from God Himself, usually the first statement out of their mouth is, "I can't forgive them, you don't know what they did to me." Don't set this book down because of what I am about to tell you but, you're right. You can't forgive. Does that really surprise you? You and I can't remember where we just put our car keys, or what we had for lunch last Wednesday, but we can sure recite every hurtful word spoken to us 30 years ago. We just don't remember those words, we hold on to those hateful words and memories. We carry them, nurse them, 30 or 40 years and some of us maybe even a lifetime. Oh, we say we have forgiven them, but let's be honest now so we can move forward and into the healing God has for us. We haven't truly forgiven anyone anything, and the first thing I want you to know about forgiveness is that you can't do it on your own! Jesus tells us this truth very plainly in one of the cornerstone verses I use in my personal daily walk with God. It can be found in John 15:5:

> "I am the vine; you are the branches. If a man remains in me and I in him, he will bear much fruit; apart from me you can do *nothing*."
> (Author's Emphasis)

Guess what *nothing* means? Just that- nothing. We can't live our marriage to the fullest, we can't raise our sons and daughters without Him, we can't have the greatest joy, we can't run our finances the best way, we can't love the way Jesus loves and we can't truly forgive without Jesus. This truth should really hit home when we think about as Jesus was dying on the cross, He was forgiving and praying for those that were killing Him even as they were laughing at His suffering. You and I say we forgive brother or sister so and so for that slander, but every time we get around them we are thinking and reliving that hurt in the back of our minds, and we still feel the sting of it in our hearts. Our forgiveness really came from pride, vanity, or in other words the flesh, which is from our own will power with the fear of God telling us we must forgive and do right. Now we are just fooling ourselves and hide it with a mask of religion. We may fool our brother and sister with that smile, but we are not fooling God. He knows the contents of our heart. True forgiveness comes from God, born of the Spirit and strengthens within and flows outward from our heart.

I want to encourage you; you can truly forgive! For that same power that was in Jesus that day to forgive his executioners, is in you richly and with all the fullness thereof and is perfecting that very thing that concerns you on a daily basis. That is, if you have accepted Christ as Lord and Savior into your heart. If you have, keep reading. But if you have not, I encourage you to accept Jesus' gift of life by now going through the prayer at the end of this chapter. You can return to where you left off. Every one of us needs Jesus.

The Secret to Forgiveness

I want to share with you a very important secret and also a rule in which we must live by on a daily basis. The *secret* of forgiveness is **realizing the forgiveness that has been given to you**. Once you truly grasp the forgiveness that is given to you on a mistake by mistake, second by second basis then you will start to understand true forgiveness and show forgiveness for others. To forgive others we must first look at ourselves. When I was in counseling classes at my school of theology we had to first look at ourselves and then face the things we had always hidden, swept under the rug, or just flat out ignored, thinking they were water under the bridge and long gone. Wounds and hurts just don't dissolve or go away because of time, and to God they all happened just a second ago. *We* must be healed before we can heal others. I was taught hurting people *hurt* people; but healed people help hurting people.

Before we learn how to forgive others and process our hurts and wounds, we must really look at ourselves before we can move on. We will start from the very words of Jesus himself in Matthew 7:3, "Why do you look at the speck of sawdust in your brother's eye and pay no attention to the plank in your own eye?" Jesus is saying "don't look at anyone else's faults or mistakes until you look at yourself and what you have done first".

Then Jesus goes on to say in verse 4 and 5:

> How can you say to your brother, 'Let me take the speck out of your eye.' You hypocrite, first take the plank out of your *own* eye, and then you will see clearly to remove the speck from your brother's eye."
> (Author's Emphasis)

I have emphasized the word *own* in that verse. Jesus said we must look at ourselves first. The first 3 chapters of this book are for dealing with ourselves; the rest are for processing and healing the wounds that have been done to us. Don't short circuit the healing God has for you by just skimming these chapters. We must take a good and *hard* look at ourselves first before we can be healed of our wounds. To do this, be honest with yourself and face the things the Holy Spirit brings to your mind and deal with those things of the past you need to be healed of.

What is the plank in my own eye? Let me give you an example. My friend Jerry and I were in my car heading out to lunch the other day and across the street was an old building they were tearing down. Overnight, vandals had spray painted graffiti all over the walls. It disgusted me that people do that, and I asked Jerry, "Hey man, look, what makes people do that? "What is going through their minds when they are vandalizing someone's property like that?" I shook my head in disgust and looked over at him for his answer. Jerry had his head lowered in shame. He replied humbly and softly, "I can't say anything, I used to do that myself." He then took a second and thought deeply then replied, "I guess in my mind I was rebelling against authority." I felt embarrassed; I didn't think that was going to be the answer when I put my righteous foot in my mouth. "Oh" was my reply.

Later that day the Holy Spirit reminded me of something I had long forgot about. He showed me and reminded me of the time when I was young and I went out to the woods on government-owned property and spray painted all the trees with the name of a gang I was trying to form. Then the Holy Spirit said, "Oh, you forgot about that didn't you? So tell me, what was going through *your* mind?" Humbled and again embarrassed, I thought to myself, and then I remembered it was the same as Jerry's-- rebellion against authority.

I thought I already knew the lesson well that I am about

to teach you, but every now and again I need a friendly reminder. Thank you Holy Spirit.

Romans 2:1

You, therefore, have no excuse, you who pass judgment on someone else, for at whatever point you judge the other, you are condemning yourself, because you who pass judgment do the same things. ~ Apostle Paul

You see, it's so easy to point at someone else and look at their faults or judge them according to their actions, but I have a harsh reality for you that most people have yet to realize, and it's a hard truth. And that truth is this: every mistake or sin we can accuse our brother or sister of doing, we have done ourselves! I usually say we, or our, to sugar coat the medicine of truth, but for this to really hit home and for you to really grasp it, I am going to personalize it. Here it is again. Every sin *you* can point to your brother for doing, you have done the same thing! Oh no? Take a moment and think about that. We think someone robbing a bank is a scum of the earth, a no-good bank robber and a thief. However let me ask you, have you ever taken anything without asking permission from whom it belonged? Even something small such as a paperclip from work? I have, and guess what that makes me. A thief. In whose eyes? God's. Oh no, those people that rob banks are the so called "bad people." I have another revelation for you; there is no difference in God's eyes from stealing a paperclip or stealing from the bank. Stealing is a sin no matter if it was the money at the bank or taking your mother's dishwashing detergent without asking. Then we somehow validate and excuse what we have done in our minds. A sin is a sin and just one separates you from God, and no amount of self justification can validate sin. Let's look at our forefather Adam.

A Chip off the Old Block

Adam sinned against God and then tried to validate it by saying, "It was the woman *you* gave me Lord!" Oh, now it's not *Adam's* fault, it's Eve's because *she* gave the forbidden fruit to him and it's God's fault for making the woman to begin with. Somehow it always turns out to be God's fault. We always try to validate our sins, *I stole it because they charge too much for it anyway, I'm having an affair because my husband doesn't listen to me anyway, I'm stealing from work because they owe me. It's okay to overcharge those that are wealthy, they are rich and can afford it, it's okay to rob that store, I'm feeding my children.*

Next question, have you ever told a lie? Something that was not true? I have, that makes me a liar. "Oh, but I have told only a few lies," If someone would ask me if I thought I told lies I would say, no of course not. Who would? If I have spoken a false statement, then I am a liar. Let's personalize it again. Ever told a lie, or something that was not true? Remember, withholding the truth is also the same as lying. Of course you have, guess what that makes you?

Oh, but we don't think of ourselves that way, but we can point a righteous finger at our brother. Jesus said to look at ourselves first. Still not convinced? Here is another one. Ever committed adultery? No?, have you ever lusted after someone? I have, and according to Jesus, in Matthew 5: 28, *"Anyone who looks at a woman lustfully has already committed adultery with her in his heart."* Guess what I am? An adulterer. And ladies, the same principle applies to you too. Have you ever lusted after another man? If you have, that makes you an adulterer too.

Here is another revelation for you. No sin is greater than another. We like to elevate one sin more than another in our eyes, but our eyes are not the ones that matter. It's God's and He is the only one qualified to judge. I want to give you an example of one sin that I hear elevated the most. The preacher bangs his fist on the podium and proclaims, "Homosexuality is a sin," yet he does so with his belly hanging over his belt. You see, gluttony is a sin too. You can have a glass of wine with your meal but indulging in wine is a sin, you can eat the right food but overindulge in it, and it's a sin. What's worst? Defiling the temple of the Lord through sexual sin, or poisoning it on a daily basis with eating the wrong things? Do you want to know the basis of this doctrine? First the word tells us in Romans 3:23 whether we are Jew or Gentile, we have all sinned and fallen short of the glory of God. Notice it grouped all sins together and didn't differentiate between us or each sin. But more importantly the basis lies with the life and ministry of Jesus, the Holy Lamb of God without spot or blemish. If Jesus would have committed just one sin, like stealing a pen from work, told a single lie or committed a "big sin" like robbing Israel's First Savings & Loan, He would not have been the Holy Lamb of God without *spot* or *wrinkle*, and His sacrifice would have been in vain. But Glory be to God! He has delivered you and I from this body of death!

Here's The Good News!

Okay, I know that was tough, and if you really were paying attention and being honest with yourself that should have stung. *Medicine usually tastes bad,* but we need it when we are sick. We must *always* look at ourselves first. Now for some great news, Jesus was tempted on all points as we are, and He *was, and still is* the Holy Lamb of God without spot and blemish! He took your sins and died in your place! He died so you and I could live. He took even those secret sins you thought no one knew about and got away with. The part that blows my mind is He died knowing how I truly am, and died for me even when I was His enemy. Romans 5:8 says He showed His love for us by dying for us and we did not deserve it. We need to stop and grasp that truth. Let that sink in. You and I didn't deserve it. However, **we** have been forgiven so he wants us to forgive others the same way (Romans 3:12). It's not right for us to be forgiven, yet we withhold our forgiveness from others. You have sinned and been forgiven; forgive as He also forgave you.

What is the secret to forgiveness? **It's realizing the forgiveness that has been given to you!** I have found when we are becoming judgmental of each other, it's because we are forgetting that fundamental truth. God is saying, "It's time to come back to solid truth," It's time to forgive; it's time to be about our Father's business, for the time is short! I want to end this chapter with a personal commentary from one of my all time favorite stories from the Bible. It directly relates to what we just went over, and it's about understanding and acknowledging who we are and what we have done, the forgiveness we have received and the love for others it produces. It's the account of when Jesus was invited over to Simon Iscariot's house, a Pharisee and Judas's father, and has His feet anointed by a woman that was known to prostitute herself. Now you have no doubt heard this was Mary Magdalene, but I want to point out this story is one of the few that appears in all four of the gospels and in all four not one time does it mention her by name. Is it Mary? Could be, but there is a reason her name is not given, God doesn't want you to tie Mary's characteristics and personality to this event. He doesn't want her singled out. It doesn't matter what her name is, she was a sinner. This is a general type and shadow or a symbolic form of someone that represents you and I. In other words, she represents the body of Christ. There's a chance it wasn't Mary. Women were often divorced from their husbands and usually for no good reason, so women were outcast and disregarded as nothing and had nowhere to go and wouldn't be hired, so many were forced to sell themselves so they could buy food. Sounds like nothing has changed since then.

This account is the one recorded by Luke in Chapter 7. Jesus is reclining at the table and a woman who lived a sinful life brought an alabaster jar of perfume and she stood behind Him at His feet weeping, wetting His feet with her tears and drying them with her hair. She then sacrificed something dear to her and poured out her expensive gift on Him in a show of love and gratitude. In verse 39, Simon is thinking to himself, but *Jesus hears what his heart is saying.* Simon thought, "If this man were a prophet, he would know who is touching him and what kind of woman she is - that she is a sinner." Simon's attitude is, "she is the sinner not me" That thinking falls in line with self-proclaimed righteousness and even the religious thinking of today. Simon is judging her from a stand point that he is in right with God because he follows religious rules and laws. He doesn't even know the only one that is righteous and has the power and authority to judge or give righteousness is sitting across from him. Jesus heard Simon and responds to him in verse 40, "Simon, I have something to tell you."

Now I want you to grasp this. The very Word of God, *the very one* from the beginning that said, "Let there be light" and formed man from the dust of the ground, is now in your house, sitting at your table and staring you right in the face and proclaims, " I have something to say to you!" Simon says, "Tell me, teacher."

Jesus gives him an example of a great debt and forgiveness of that debt. It goes like this starting in verse 41, "Two men owed money to a certain moneylender. One owed him five hundred denarii, and the other fifty. Neither of them had the money to pay him back, so he canceled the debts of both. Now which of them will love him more?" Simon gives the correct answer, "I suppose the one who had the bigger debt canceled." "You have judged correctly," Jesus said. In other words, the one that realized the forgiveness of his own debt (sin) that was stacked against him was the one that was more thankful. His attitude is different. This revelation that we were a sinner and enemy of God and had a debt that was canceled only by the sacrifice of Jesus should always be on our minds and engraved on the tablet of our hearts. Also notice that both the fifty denarii debt (paper clip stolen) or the greater five hundred denarii debt (robbed a bank) are amounts which can't be paid but receive the same forgiveness in the eyes of God and could only be canceled by Him (the lender) alone.

Let's continue. Jesus is about to hand Simon a *true* righteous judgment. He uses a person the rest of the world counted as worthless and a sinner to prove this point. Jesus said, "Do you see this woman? I came into your house. You did not give me any water for my feet, but she wet my feet with her tears and wiped them with her hair. You did not give me a kiss, but this woman, from the time I entered, has not stopped kissing my feet. You did not put oil on my head, but she has poured perfume on my feet. Therefore, I tell you, her many sins have been forgiven-for she loved much. But he who has been forgiven little loves little."

Jesus breaks down the comparison between Simon and her. You did this, she did this, you did this, she did this... the difference between the two is they are both sinners but one realized the debt that has been forgiven her, and the other has not. One has her sins forgiven and is washed clean because of her *faith* in Christ. She acknowledges what she's done and doesn't rationalize or excuse it. She doesn't say to herself, "I only sold myself a time or two, that doesn't make me a prostitute" or "I needed money for food." She first acknowledges her sins, next the forgiveness given to her, and then she loves, because she knows and acknowledges the forgiveness that was given to her. The other thinks he is righteous and points the finger at others. He then shows little love because he minimizes his own sins. Jesus then turns to the woman and assures her, "Your faith has saved you; go in peace." He does this because He wants everyone to know righteousness and forgiveness does not come by works but by faith. One person is now justified (through faith) and forgiven, but one is not (because of works and the law).

Lord, give us the wisdom and understanding in the

forgiveness you give to us! Let us grasp and understand the forgiveness that has been given to us. Let us always keep on our minds the love You show us and teach us how to love the way You love us! Teach us to forgive others the way You forgive us! Teach us to show mercy to each other the way You continually show us mercy.

If you have not accepted forgiveness for your sins through faith in Jesus Christ, there is only one way to do that and that is through the sacrifice made for us by Jesus when He died on the cross for our sins. If you have never accepted Jesus before, or if after reading about the forgiveness you have been given, you wish to renew your relationship with your first love, Jesus Christ, pray this prayer with me.

Lord Jesus,

I want to bow my head to your Holiness and I want to thank you for forgiving me and loving me while I was yet a sinner. I take this time to stop and ponder your goodness and mercy. Renew my salvation by filling my heart up with your Holy Spirit and come into my life and forgive me of my sins. Wash me clean with Your righteousness and teach me Your ways. I have been judgmental of others but now I have taken a good look at myself and realize I need Your love and forgiveness in my heart and life. Teach me to love others as You love me. Teach me to forgive the way You forgive me. Come into my life and change me and make me like You. I love You and put my trust in You. I thank You for my salvation! Amen.

CHAPTER

2

JUDGE NOT!
FORGIVING AND JUDGING

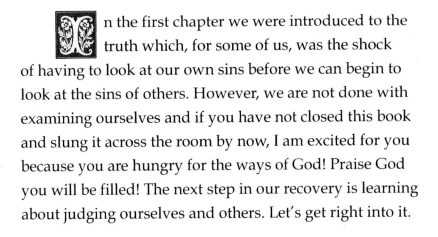n the first chapter we were introduced to the truth which, for some of us, was the shock of having to look at our own sins before we can begin to look at the sins of others. However, we are not done with examining ourselves and if you have not closed this book and slung it across the room by now, I am excited for you because you are hungry for the ways of God! Praise God you will be filled! The next step in our recovery is learning about judging ourselves and others. Let's get right into it.

**The weight of our judgment for one another
is the same weight God uses for us.**

In other words, the same measure you use to judge others, God will take that *same* measure and *apply* it to you! Jesus says this Himself in Matthew 7:1-2:

> "Do not judge, or you will be judged. For in the same way you judge others, you will be judged, and the measure you use, it will be measured to you."

Wow! How could we as Christians miss and overlook this very powerful statement. The NKJ says it like this, "Judge not, that you be not judged. For what judgment you judge, you will be judged; and with the *same* measure you use, it will be measured back to you." (Author's Emphasis)

I say again, wow!, not just because of the weight of the content but the fact I have never heard this mentioned or preached in any church nor lived out from any man. I will never forget the day God showed me this revelation and I want to share it with you right now. Read very carefully and know this. **God takes whatever weapon we use against each other and turns it right back on the one using the weapon!** Listen to David acknowledge this fact in these Psalms:

"The nations have fallen into the pit they have dug; their feet are caught in the net they have hidden" (Psalm 9:15)

"They spread a net for my feet- I was bowed down in distress. They dug a pit in my path- but they have fallen into it themselves. Selah (Psalm 57:6)

and again **"Since they hid their net for me without cause and without cause dug a pit for me, may ruin overtake them by surprise- may the net they hid entangle them, may they fall into the pit, to their ruin."** Psalm 35:7-8

If anyone shoots an arrow of slander towards anyone, God takes that very arrow and bends it into a boomerang and sends it right back to the one that sent it. That is God's way of doing things and you can say it's His

M.O. or profile. God doesn't counter with His weapon. He just uses the weapon of those that seek destruction. Whatever weapon you use, God turns it right back on you, and uses the same measure in which it was used. When Peter used a sword in the garden of Gethsemane, Jesus immediately told him, "Put your sword back in its place. For all who draw the sword will die by the sword."

Are you catching on yet? Here are more examples revealed to me by the Holy Spirit. Goliath was killed not by a sling and stone but by a sword, his *own* sword, the one he tried to kill David with. Daniel's accusers tried to get him thrown into the lion's den but God saved him and guess who the lions did eat. Daniel's *accusers* along with their whole family! In the book of Esther, Haman plotted to destroy the Jews and even built a hanging gallows seventy-five feet high in which to hang them. God intervened and not one Jew was hung but guess who was. Haman on his *own* contraption! It was recorded in the book of Daniel the third chapter that Shadrach, Meshach and Abednego escaped the fiery furnace unharmed but it's recorded that the soldiers that built the fire and threw them in it were the ones killed. It was Pharaoh's own pride that kept the children of Israel in bondage and it was that very pride God used to lure him into the midst of the ocean, resulting in his death.

But wait Jason, those are examples of the wicked coming against God's people. God doesn't do that to His children. If you take a look again at Matthew 7:1 you will see Jesus is talking to everybody, you and me. Whatever measure we use, it comes back to us. Whatever we sow we reap, period. We sow to the flesh, we reap the flesh, we sow to the spirit we reap the spirit. So whatever we sow either good or bad that is what we reap. God gives us a chance in every situation to either show mercy, or to condemn ourselves. Remember Proverbs 18:21 says, "The tongue has the power of life and death, and those who love it will eat its fruit." So it *is* better to **judge not**, and we are never anymore like Jesus as when we show mercy.

Go and learn what this means:
"I desire mercy, not sacrifice." ~ Jesus
(Matt 9:13)

I want to share with you a prime example of God's "boomerang judgment" on someone that is dear to His heart. It's King David, and in 2 Samuel Chapter 11 David is coveting Uriah's wife and plots to kill him so he can have her. Uriah is a faithful soldier under the King's command and David orders Joab, captain of the army, to send Uriah to the front of battle. Uriah is killed and Joab sends word back to David, and this is David's response to the message in verse 25, "Say this to Joab: "Don't let this upset you; the sword devours one as well as another."

About a year later the Lord sends his prophet Nathan to David to confront him and hand him judgment. Always remember God gives us a chance to repent from our heart and turn from sin. He gives us a chance to judge ourselves, and show mercy before he is forced to correct us out of love. However, David has not repented and is so callous with sin that his heart is no longer sensitive to the spirit. David doesn't realize the subject of Nathan's story is him. Nathan tells David a parable of a rich man taking from a poor man his one and only lamb. After the parable, David gets a chance to repent and show mercy, but instead his anger (self-righteousness and judgment) is aroused and he speaks his own judgment. Listen to David's response," As surely as the Lord lives, the man who did this deserves to die! He must pay for that lamb four times over, because he did such a thing and had no pity."

Can you see how David was blind to his own sins and was ready to judge others for theirs? Can you see that when we sin we want a pass and when someone else sins we want justice? In every situation, God gives us a chance to do right and even correct ourselves, however David would not. Let's find out the Lord's response and what happened to David. We will pick it up in verse 9. Nathan is saying,

"Why did you despise the word of the Lord by doing evil in his eyes? You struck down Uriah the Hittite with the sword and took his wife to be your own. You killed him with the sword of the Ammonites. Now therefore, the sword will never depart from your house, because you despised me and took the wife of Uriah the Hittite to be your own."

So in other words, David used the sword, and the sword is come back to him. It was permanent in Uriah's life, it's now permanent in David's life. Nathan is not finished yet, let's hear the rest of the judgment.

"Out of your own household I am going to bring calamity upon you. Before your very eyes, I will take your wives and give them to one who is close to you, and he will lie with your wives in broad daylight. You did it in secret, but I will do this thing in broad daylight before all Israel."

Here lies another way of God; he crucifies people in the open, not privately. Pay close attention to the actions and judgment of King David and the actions and judgments of the Lord God; they mirror each other. In the two scripture passages above the Lord personalizes the actions to David (*you* did this, *your* house, *your* wife) 14 times! God judged the weight of David's sin and applied it back to him. Then David said to Nathan, "I have sinned against the Lord." God forgave David of his sins but his sins brought consequences. Here lies part of our problem. We think when Jesus died on the cross and forgave us of our sins we have a license to do what we want, and God looks the other way, or sweeps it under the rug. We don't say that but for the most part, that's how we live, and that's how it looks to God. Our freedom is not a license to sin! My friend we deceive ourselves! Always remember God will not be mocked for whatever a man sows that he will also reap (Galatians 6:7).

You Fool!
"But I say to you that whoever is angry with his brother without cause shall be in danger of the judgment. And

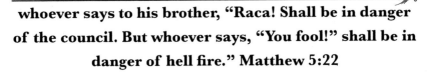

whoever says to his brother, "Raca! Shall be in danger of the council. But whoever says, "You fool!" shall be in danger of hell fire." Matthew 5:22

God weighs our heart and either rewards us or disciplines us using the intent of our heart as the deciding factor in the scale of judgment. In Matthew 5:22, Jesus warns us about esteeming our self-righteousness above our brother in the way of loftiness, and pointing the finger of judgment. This is what is meant by *without cause* in verse 21. He compares physical murder to an act tried openly in court; however, in verse 22 judging our brother without a cause will bring us in danger of hell fire, or *Gehenna*, which was an infamous place of forbidden religious practices by the former Kings of Judah. Jeremiah, the prophet, spoke of it's impending judgment and doom by God. Gehenna, became known as a term in Jesus' day as a common reminder of God's judgment. Kind of like when we use Sodom and Gomorrah today. In other words, when Jesus said you're in danger of hell fire He means, "You are in danger of God's judgment." It also means don't start pointing your finger at your brother, or you will be accused by God of unlawful religious practices! However unlike us, God's judgment is always fair and equally balanced.

Who are we to judge another?

There is a common practice among Christians I have

seen my whole life; it's never spoken of, but you and I are quite aware of it. We start to believe the righteousness we acquire through the death and resurrection of Jesus entitles us to judge each other. We must always keep this in check. Not only is that doctrine of I'm- now-holy-and-better–than-you not true, but righteousness is never self-generated. In other words, any righteousness we have comes from God and God only. I say again, righteousness is never self-generated. Not in works, not in deeds, not by the Law, but by faith in Christ whose *own* life and death entitles us to be saved through trusting in Him. However as we start to mature along in our walk we are prone to let our guard down and start to think of ourselves greater than we ought to. We *are* redeemed and God's chosen people; however, we are ordered to stay humble and meek before God (1Peter 5:5).

Better to be of a humble spirit with the lowly, than to divide the spoil with the proud (Proverbs 16:19).

We are saved not by anything we have done but by God's grace. Before we asked Jesus to come into our heart, our righteousness was filthy rags. Fifty years later we have matured spiritually yet *our* righteousness is still filthy rags. But Jesus' righteousness is our salvation. Our newly found freedom in Christ should never be an excuse to bind others in religious rhetoric taught by man. God said, Judge NOT! He is the righteous judge and the only one qualified to judge. Listen to what James wrote in Chapter 4 verse 11 in his epistle:

"Do not speak evil of one another, brethren. He who speaks evil of a brother and judges his brother, speaks evil of the law and judges the law. But if you judge the law, you are not a doer of the law but a judge. There is one Lawgiver, who is able to save and to destroy. Who are you to judge another?"

James says, do not speak evil of someone else, there's one lawgiver and only one qualified to judge the law. We are to be doers of the Law, not judges of the law. I will never forget the day God showed me that every sin I have pointed to someone else as doing, I have done the same thing! Have I stolen? Have I told a lie? Have I let someone down? Have I committed adultery? Have I broken promises? Have I said things in anger? Have I wounded others with my tongue? Certainly yes to all these and of the latter I am chief! Thank God for His mercy!

The apostle Paul devotes almost an entire chapter in Romans to this very subject. Listen to some of these excerpts from Chapter 2:

V.1 Therefore you are inexcusable, O man whoever you are who judge, for in whatever you judge another you condemn yourself; for you who judge, practice the same things! V.3 And do you think this, O man, you who judge those practicing such things, and doing the same, that you will escape the judgment of God?

Peter speaks of the judgment of God as well in 1 Peter 4:17, "It is time for judgment to begin at the house of God." The house is not the church you're attending; it is you! You're the house of God! God judges His children first! God judges His children then disciplines them; the wicked, God judges, and then *punishes* them. Let's look at more of Paul's letter to the Romans. In Chapter 2, when confronting Jews who point a finger at Gentiles Paul says:

V.21 You, therefore, who teach another, do you teach yourself? You who preach that a man should not steal, do you steal?

V.22 You who say, "Do not commit adultery," do you commit adultery? You who abhor idols, do you rob temples?

Always remember this, when dealing with the sin of idols the biggest one is ourself. My friend I hope this truth is setting in. We have been judging others with no righteousness of our own. We wear lofty attitudes on our sleeves. We have been pointing fingers at others from the stand point of they're the ones in the wrong. Our attitude consciences consist of the thoughts, "I may sin once in a while but *those* over there are 'the bad people'." We cover ourselves with fig leaves of religion and hide behind a false mask of humility. We shouldn't live the law from the outside and point the finger at those we feel aren't like us; we are required to live the law from our hearts with a clean conscience and humility in Christ. Our conscience will either condemn us or free us as we prepare for the day the Lord God will judge the secrets of men by Jesus Christ. (Romans 2:16)

Now let's put what we have just learned to some real life scenarios.

It was a Friday evening and I walked into the office of Vivian, my good friend, counselor and mentor. I had a late afternoon appointment and as I walked in she started with a question. "Jason I want to ask you something, I want your opinion." I said, "Okay, shoot," as I sat down. She started her question. "There is a woman who is a new Christian and a single mother. She has no skills or degrees and she is working as an exotic dancer at night. She is feeling pressured by other Christians at church to quit her job. What do you think she should do?" The first thing that popped in my mind was, *Why would I get asked this question about someone else's life and making their own decisions?* Also, *what does that have to do with me?* In other words, I was thinking, *I'm not her, why would I tell her what she should do?* I didn't have to think about it even for a second. I quickly threw my hands up in a "what" gesture and replied, "I don't know what she should do, I'm not her, I'm not in her shoes or her place." "Right!" replied Vivian and a smile began to spread across her cheeks. "That, my friend, is the right answer." I then learned she had asked that question to every one she met that day and I was the only one with the right answer. She said everyone told this girl she was in sin and to quit her job and that was not even a question to consider. But not one of them were willing to help her out financially nor did they have any solution to what she should do to pay her bills. Study James 2:16.

I must admit I felt good inside and maybe even a little proud that I answered the question correctly. Mainly, I was joyful to see the work the Holy Spirit had been working in me and the changes he has made. For if I was asked that same question just a few years ago, I would have answered the same way as everyone else and maybe thought long and hard, searching my mind through my own wisdom and experiences or scriptures to build a case against her. However that to me was an easy one, I don't judge her, I'm not in her shoes, I don't know all her circumstances and I don't have her solutions. Only God does. I have learned to keep quiet and seek what God is saying first and listen to His instructions. Anything else would be drawn from my own experience and knowledge of the scriptures. Before you think that Vivian and I condone exotic dancing or any other sin for that matter, think again. Is taking your clothes off for money and prostituting God's body a sin? Yes. Do I support it, excuse it or say it's okay because she is a single mother and needs the money? No.

However, let's put together and put to use the knowledge we have learned from these first two chapters. What's the difference between exotic dancing and stealing from your workplace? Remember James 4:11, "who are you to judge another?" There is only one law giver and one judge of the law! It's the Lord. It's not body-made-of-dirt, can't-even-save-his-own-self Jason. It's not the I-attend-church-Holier-than-thou-self -appointed-judge-of-what-is-right-and-wrong church-goer. It's not the I'm-without-sin-so-here-comes-a-rock hypocrite. Two thousand years ago Jesus said, "Let him who is without sin cast the first stone." That still applies to you and I today.

As we end this chapter I will give you another real life scenario and I want you to see if you can now spot the red flags.

Mary is a housewife and is watching the Atlanta Braves on television as she is folding her laundry and talking to Susan, her friend from church, on the phone. Mary sees the Braves' third baseman, Chipper Jones, and says to Susan, "I hate that Chipper Jones, I used to like him, until he cheated on his wife, now I just can't stand to look at him. I just can't support him anymore. And I'll tell you who else I can't stand. Cindy, in the choir, yep, everybody knows her husband is in Iraq and last night John saw her sitting in the window of Barnes & Nobles having coffee with James from the praise team. I hope that girl gets caught."

How many red flags do you suppose have popped up here?
Gossip? Slander? Meddling in the affairs of others? Judging? Sentencing? Hatred? Speaking curses over people? While Mary is guilty of conducting all this and more she is judging from her limited point of view and lack of understanding. She doesn't know or consider the

ramification of her comments and how God is really judging, witnessing and overseeing this entire drama. Worse still, she is spreading it to Susan so that it spills over into her heart as well. What a tangled web of ignorance we weave!

For our own clarification, Mary doesn't know Chipper Jones, except who she sees on T.V. and Cindy from the praise team, whose husband is serving in Iraq, was going over words for a new song with two other praise team members. As John drove by and did *his* judging, he didn't see Linda, because she was in the bathroom and worship leader Pastor Barry was standing in line waiting to order a mocha.

My friend in Christ, I hope God has revealed something to you on the inside of you while you read this chapter. I hope God has removed that veil of deceit from judging others and the weight of self-righteousness from your heart. May we now learn the way God sees us and always view others the way God views others. Let us be quick to show mercy. Let us be quick to listen and slow to speak. May we always watch what we say and guard every word that comes from our mouth. We will eat the fruit in which we have sown. When our eye becomes wicked and quick to judge others or form our own opinion by what we see, may we always remember the Words of the King, "Judge Not."

If the Holy Spirit has revealed to you some times or situations you have been critical of others, and spoken foolishly as we all have before, you can denounce those things right now and repent as David did and let God wash your conscience clean with His Holiness and Righteousness. Maybe you have judged people with tattoos, or those of a different skin color. Maybe you withheld your blessing from someone who has gone through a divorce. What ever it may be, God is always faithful and delights to show mercy. Let's go to Him now.

Jesus,

Thank you for showing me I have been critical of others. I have been judging others and I have learned that you alone are the True Judge and the only one qualified to judge. Help me never to judge others but keep in mind you are the judge. I am sorry for speaking against others (or say their name) and I ask you to forgive me and wash my conscience clean. I want to see people the way you see them and show everyone the same mercy you have shown to me. You are my righteousness and my salvation and I put my trust in you. Teach me your ways and guide me in your truth. Amen.

CHAPTER

3

PRIDE: THE ROOT OF UNFORGIVENESS

God resists the proud, but gives grace to the humble.
1 Peter 5:5

othing will separate you quicker from the
very presence of God than pride. Pride is
the mother of hell. It separated Lucifer from his title and
position in heaven and no place was found for him. Jesus
Himself said, *"I saw him fall like lightning from heaven"* (*Luke 10:18*).
Pride is firmly rooted and lives in disobedience to God and
comes against the knowledge, ways and commandments
of God.

Pride is our first and biggest hurdle to overcome
if we are to learn how to forgive and **pride is the root of
unforgiveness**. A root is first a seed that is planted, in this
case *inflicted on us* (a wound), that results in bitterness and
resentfulness. This seed takes root in our heart and grows
to yield fruit of disobedience towards God. This root that
yields bitter fruit in the mouth of God not only keeps us
from experiencing God's best for us, but it defiles others
too. Pride keeps us from experiencing God's grace and
puts up a wall that alienates us from fellowship from our

fellow brethren. Yes, it is possible to miss God's grace! Hebrews 12:15 says, *See to it that no one misses the grace of God and that no bitter root grows up to cause trouble and defile many.*

By withholding our forgiveness towards others because of pride, we are just separating ourselves from the provision of God our Father. Don't be fooled; we can miss God's grace. Look at Proverbs 11:2, *When pride comes, then comes disgrace, but with humility comes wisdom.* What does it say happens when pride comes? Disgrace. Look at the letters in disgrace: dis-Grace. The prefix "dis-" means to take away. "Grace" is the substance of God's love filling in our weaknesses when we strive and fall short. We have God's grace and then it is taken away because of pride. Next, look at what it says humility brings. Wisdom! Wisdom is not found in a book nor can it be taught in class. Wisdom is a person! Wisdom is Jesus Christ. So humility brings more of Jesus' character and nature in our life which includes His provision during our toughest trials. Nothing can be plainer than 1Peter 5:5 *God resists the proud but gives grace to the humble.*

What is Pride?

The fear of the Lord is to hate evil;
I hate pride and arrogance, evil behavior and perverse speech.
Proverbs 8:13

Webster's New World Dictionary defines pride as A. *an over high opinion of oneself;* B. *haughtiness; arrogance.* If I asked 10 self-confessed Christians at random if they consider themselves to be a prideful person according to Webster's definition, I bet 8 out of 10 would say *they are not prideful* and may even consider themselves a humble person. They deceive themselves. I can boldly make that statement because I know them by their fruit and how they respond to God's personal invitations of intimacy with Him and how they respond to others around them. However, the most important definition of pride and the one that really needs to concern us are not from Webster's Dictionary but from God's. The main scripture this is based on is from a Psalm of David:

> In his pride the wicked does not seek him;
> In all his thoughts there is no room for God.
> His ways are always prosperous; he is
> haughty and your laws are far from him; He
> sneers at all his enemies. Psalm 10: 4-5

Pride is when we take God out of the equation and make no room for Him. Pride says, "I don't need God." Pride says, "I can do this on my own." Pride says, "I really don't have a problem." Pride says, "I haven't done anything and I don't need help." Pride says, "Everything I have I have gotten myself!" Pride says to God, "I am doing just fine on my own and I really don't need to acknowledge You right now." Pride is a standpoint of pointing the finger at everyone else while you say to yourself, "I'm okay".

Pride is **always** associated with the wicked in the Bible. It **always** represents the opposing side of what God says. Pride comes from within our heart and according to our Lord that is what defiles a man. Jesus said in Mark 7:22, "What comes out of a man makes him unclean. For within, out of men's hearts come evil thoughts, sexual immorality, theft, murder, adultery, greed, malice, deceit, lewdness, envy, slander, **pride** and folly."
(Author's emphasis)
You may ask yourself, "Have I ever been prideful like that?" Well, let's test this thing out now.

One Sunday the Holy Spirit is really moving in your church and instructs the Pastor to call to the altar all those that have a problem with anger. The Pastor opens the altar and *you don't go* even though you know you are battling anger at home and at work, and you know the Holy Spirit was speaking to *you* during the service. Oh how your heart burns and aches to be set free from the bondage you feel only you know about. You know God is talking to you; you know that it was *you* the Holy Spirit was directly speaking to. You feel the burning in your heart to step out from behind the chair and go, but you don't because you are afraid of what people may think! You are a well respected Christian among your fellow brothers and sisters and you are afraid of what they will think of you. You are already imagining it in your head, your stepping out into the aisle and heading up front, with all the eyes seeming to be on you. You can feel their whispers and judgments filling your head and breathing down your back. You now begin to rationalize and reason away the Holy Spirit and talk yourself out of it. You say to yourself. *I really don't need help. I'm okay. Just give it more time, I can do it. I can do this on my own. I really don't need to go down there. I can work this out myself tomorrow.* Meanwhile the Holy Spirit is calling you. You don't go and there is a mighty move of God and all those around you that went to the altar and took God at His Word were miraculously healed. But not you, you kept your head down and held tight the wooden chair in front of you. You just missed God. You missed your healing, you missed your blessing, you missed God's grace, and you were disobedient to God when He called out to you. Guess why? **Pride**.

Who hasn't done this before? I know I have many times. However, I no longer do. If an altar call applies to me and my Master says to my heart "Come!", I'm going, *period*. But there was a time in my life when I held a leadership role in the area of altar counseling and I would sometimes need to be the one going for help. But I would hold back afraid of what people thought of me. I was afraid people would see I was really naked and looking for God's touch and presence. Years ago, God called out to Adam who was hiding behind a tree, "Where are you?" God knew where Adam was physically, God wanted to point out to Adam for Adam's sake where Adam was! Adam's reply was, "I heard you, and I was afraid because I was naked. So I hid myself." God is still calling out to us and we are still hiding and are afraid of people seeing our nakedness. We are still hiding ourselves behind the tree of wood when God calls. Only this time it's a wooden pew or chair.

At those altar call times, when the minister's message is really hitting home, God is calling to us and in His great Love, God is pointing out where we are **for our sake** so we won't be removed from the greatest pleasure of all-- His presence. And we answer God by telling Him, "I'm fine, I really don't miss your presence. I can do this myself and I'd rather stay here separated from you than have my nakedness and dependence on You exposed." The truth is we are all naked and we all need God, no one is exempt. Like Adam found out, our decision to hide ourselves and to point our finger at others when exposed can get us in hot water with our Father God real quick. I said it before, I will say it again. Nothing will separate you from the intimacy and presence of God quicker than your pride. If we are going to get back into the sanctuary of God's presence we have to let go of our centered pride and obey the voice of God when He calls on us.

Pride can keep you from your forgiveness.

Pride will hinder our intimacy with God on a personal level first. It can also be just as damaging when we won't forgive someone because we refuse to let go. That is when pride affects our ability to forgive, again tying God's hands so that He is helpless to help us on our behalf.

Now, as one that serves in a minister's position, I have witnessed brothers and sisters in Christ come up to the altar for healing and the Holy Spirit will prompt me to ask if they have anyone they need to forgive in their heart. Many times they say immediately, "Oh yes, I sure do!" If they are willing to forgive, we go through a repentance and forgiveness prayer and the release is so wonderful. Now they are ready to receive from God, and they always do. However, if they shake their head "no" and are not open to forgiving that person or situation we have a spiritual fight on our hands, because unforgiveness operates in the flesh not the spirit. Pride and unforgiveness are characteristics born of the flesh and create enmity between you and God the Spirit. Refusing to forgive someone and holding on to grudges and past hurts is rooted in pride and is like **slowly drinking poison ourselves and hoping the offending person dies**. Withholding our blessing is deep-rooted in pride and we believe that holding on to our blessing is hurting those that hurt us. We are only hurting ourselves! Forgiving each other is a major staple in our Christian walk and principle of Christ. If you are called to follow Christ and want a close relationship with God, you must forgive. The *first* person to benefit from forgiveness is the person doing the forgiving! God can remove all the bitter poison from your heart that has held you from His presence and experiencing the total joy of your salvation. Healing and forgiveness depend and start with you, not the offender. It's not the offender's responsibility to make things right between you and God. Each and every one of us is responsible for our own actions and for our own relationship with God, and He commands us to forgive.

Don't let pride and unforgiveness separate you from God and His wonderful presence. Many times God will not heal someone of their physical or spiritual problems because of unforgiveness in their lives. I have seen this at altar calls. God cannot bless someone or work on their behalf if He has given them an order and they refuse to obey it. Yet *they* want His help and healing. Pride ties the hand of God from moving and acting on our behalf. How could we expect God to heal us and forgive us if we will not forgive others? God will not bless disobedience. Jesus has told us very plainly and it does not get any clearer than this:

"For if you forgive men when they sin against you, your heavenly Father will also forgive you. But if you do not forgive men their sins, your Father will not forgive your sins." Matt 6:14

Forgiving each other is a *commandment* by God, not a request, Jesus said in John 14:15, "If you love me you will keep my commandments."

On this one particular occasion, a young man responded to our call for anyone wanting to receive the Holy Spirit. We prayed for Him and we asked God for the evidence of speaking in tongues. We know he received because he asked, however something seemed to block the way of the Holy Spirit from moving and showing evidence of his baptism. For several minutes, He had this puzzled look on his face. We began to pray and He sat down with his face in his hands going over his life and thinking about things asking God to help him receive. Several minutes passed. Then he began to pour out his heart to God and God showed him he had not let go of the abuse from his childhood and he began to give it to God. Then suddenly, he doubled over in his chair and fell to his face like someone had just punched him in the stomach. He began to wail deep down and quiet at first and it grew louder and louder, God was doing a miracle in this young man's life by removing all the hurt and pain caused by others in his past. He began to wail and cry uncontrollably as God removed all the hurt that was caused him, perhaps through a father or father figure or perhaps through a friend or girl that hurt him dearly. He began to praise God and his evidence of the Holy Spirit through tongues began to pour out his lips to his Redeemer and the one who has taken away his pain!

He could have held on to his hurt and wounds but he chose to let it go and give it to God. Sometimes hurts can become a stronghold around people's hearts and lives, built over many years. The wounded have carried the hurt for so long they have intimately embraced it and let the wound become a part of their lives, sometimes molding their lives around their wound (we will look at the effect on us later in the book). The thought of letting it go can be scary to them and they shake their heads, "No, I don't want to let it go, I can't." Sometimes they have lived so long with the hurt and bitterness they forgot what their life was like before they were wounded. God wants to set you free from your bitterness and heal your broken heart. One of my favorite scriptures about Jesus is found in the book of Isaiah in the first verse and it tells why Jesus came and how God feels about us, *"He has sent Me to heal the brokenhearted, To proclaim liberty to the captives, And the opening of the prison to those who are bound."* However, God will never override your free will. You have a choice, and you must choose to forgive. Don't let that hurt and bitterness continue, let it go.

Don't want to let it go?
You will find pride is at the root of unforgiveness
and the unwillingness to let go.

We secretly plan and plot our revenge to repay that someone for hurting us; however, choosing to forgive someone is giving up our right to avenge ourselves. We must come to the knowledge and understanding that we are not the judge and God said, *"Vengeance is mine. I will repay" (Romans 12:9).* When we take matters into our own hands we are acting in the place of God and we are really telling Him, "I don't trust you to handle this. You are not doing a very good job; if I were in charge I would handle this matter in this way." Our wounded pride says and sometimes even screams, "God! Didn't you see what they did to me? Why aren't you reacting? I will take matters into my own hands". Again Proverbs 20:22 says, "Do not say, 'I'll pay you back for this wrong'! Wait for the Lord, and he will deliver you."

We secretly want open and public justice for the wound we secretly have inside.

We are not to avenge ourselves but rely on God and His judgment. He is the only one I have ever found that has both sides of the story in complete form, can see the whole picture and is fully qualified to judge. After being wounded, our judgment and view is seen through the eyes of our wound, and our perception is warped and one-sided. Therefore I have learned to give God my wound so He can touch it and heal it. However choosing to forgive someone and turning our situations and hurt over to God is not only being obedient to God, you are giving up the right to avenge yourself. You may be surprised at this but in God's eyes giving justice and mercy is more important than receiving it. Jesus tells us in Matthew 5:38-41:

You have heard that it was said, Eye for eye, and tooth for tooth. But I tell you, do not resist an evil person. If someone strikes you on the right cheek, turn to him the other also. And if someone wants to sue you and take your tunic, let him have your cloak as well. If someone forces you to go one mile, go with him two miles.

What Jesus is trying to tell us is don't expect mercy

or want revenge in response to those hurting us and spitefully using us or *wounding us,* instead give to them, pray for them, show them mercy. In other words, show mercy when they don't deserve it, don't pay back wrong for wrong, hurt for hurt, wound for wound. Instead of looking for revenge for yourself, show them mercy.

God is the only righteous judge and will judge between the two persons. He will reward those who fear Him, obey Him and keep His commandments. Does this make a dent or come to any conclusions in letting go of our anger and bitterness and let God take control? If you search your heart you may find pride at the foundation of your struggles to let go and this is why. You are afraid your wounds will go unnoticed and unresolved, fearing the wound was inflicted in secret and no open justice is to be found. You secretly want open and public justice for the wound you secretly have inside.

We all have wounds and if someone inflicts damage to us our first instinct is to inflict them back. However God's ways are not our ways and our desire to retaliate is found in the weakness of our flesh. That is how we used to react when we lived like the rest of the world, without the knowledge of God and His will, but now we are in Christ and we follow His ways and commandments and we shouldn't continue to behave in the manner of the world. In order for God to heal and move on our behalf we must take action in obedience and give our hurts to God. 1Peter 5:7 says, *"Casting all your care upon Him, for He cares for you."* We must forgive in order to receive forgiveness.

God Is The Judge

I must ask this question, who can take care of this situation better, God or you? Can you heal the situation? Can you avenge better than God? Are you more qualified to judge in God's place? Are we qualified to judge fully, righteously, impartially and over the entire situation? The apostle Paul was a man that was wounded by those closest to him. Those who are brothers and sisters in Christ hurt us the most because we trust them the most. However whether they were friends or enemies of the gospel, Paul said it like this in the His first letter to the church at Corinth:

"I care very little if I am judged by you or by any human court: indeed, I do not even judge myself. My conscience is clear, but that does not make me innocent. It is the Lord who judges me. Therefore judge nothing before the appointed time; wait till the Lord comes. He will bring to light what is hidden in darkness and will expose the motives of men's hearts. At the time each will receive his praise from God." 1 Corinthians Chapter 4:3

Did you catch that? Not only is Christ the judge, but He will judge according to our actions and our motives of the heart. That judgment includes both sides. Think about that for a moment. He will judge the motives of our hearts. The true motive in our heart is something that you and I can't see about each other, however God can. So our motives and intents of the heart have weight in God's eyes. We will be judged on them. That's one of the reasons we must not take matters into our own hands. We must make sure our motives are right in our hearts or pride will sabotage us. Our pride will not let us have true motives and judge in righteousness. Not as long as we want to avenge ourselves and take matters into our own hands.

Sometimes we can even fool ourselves into thinking the justice we seek is what God intends to happen. As we end this chapter and before we move to the next one, take this moment to ask God to reveal to you the motives of your heart and if pride stands in the way of you letting go of the offense and wounds in your life. If the Holy Spirit reveals something to you, He may show you a situation, or remind you of a scripture or even speak to your heart, or He may give you quiet peace. Turn the situation over to God and let Him alone judge the situation. If He reveals in your heart your motives are rooted in pride, pray this prayer or one like it in your own words.

Father, I 'm sorry I have been holding on to the hurt wanting to avenge myself. Thank you for revealing this to me. I turn this hurt over to you and put my hope and trust fully in your hands for you to judge. I give up my right to avenge myself and trust fully in you. Thank you for showing me this, in Jesus' name. Amen.

PART TWO

UNDERSTANDING FORGIVENESS

I will instruct you in the way you should go; I will guide you with My eye.
Do not be like the horse or like the mule, which have no understanding, which
must be harnessed with bit and bridle, else they will not come near you.

~ King David (from Psalm 32:8-9)

CHAPTER

4

WHAT FORGIVENESS IS, WHAT FORGIVENESS ISN'T

To understand what God means when He commands us to forgive and understand what He is asking from us, we need to understand what forgiveness is and what it is not in the eyes of God. Forgiving does not mean reconciling our differences with one another. Now, don't get me wrong, reconciling and working things out with each other is great-- it's even scriptural (we'll look at that in a moment); but what happens when you have two people arguing and one won't agree? What if the person that has hurt you is no longer alive? These are actually quite common situations.

For example, the case of a son who was mistreated unimaginably in all areas by his father who never repented for the damage he caused to his son and then died in his sins, leaving his son understandably bitter and full of hatred. Can the son still forgive his father? Of course he can. Does he need his father's permission to receive his healing and release from God? Of course not. That's because when God asks us to forgive, He's talking to us first on an individual basis. You don't need two agreeing people to fulfill what God asks us to do in the area of forgiveness. In fact **the first person who benefits from forgiveness is the one doing the forgiving!** We forgive because we want God's forgiveness and understand we need to be forgiven.

There are several misconceptions about what forgiveness is. Most people think forgiveness equals reconciliation between two people. We think we need to deal face to face with the other person (the offender) in order to be healed or receive forgiveness. Now, there is a time you need to leave your gift at the altar and go to your brother to make things right (**Matthew 5:23**); but that is when *you* have sinned against someone yourself and the Holy Spirit reminds you that your hands are not clean. You must go first to your brother (the person offended) and ask for forgiveness. If he hears you, great! But if not, then your conscience will be clear before God. You have done what God commanded you. It doesn't matter if they *accept* your repentance, God does. You have obeyed God's commandment and you will not be held accountable. However, they will be held accountable if they do not forgive. But you must forgive and do it from your heart (**Matthew 18:35**). We need to be concerned first and foremost about being reconciled to God.

When we forgive, the first thing that gets reconciled is our standing with God. That is the secret to true reconciliation. But what if the person I offended is no longer living? What if the person that hurt *me* is no longer alive today? You see those questions go to show us forgiveness can become a reality through just one person. Reconciliation is not a commandment, forgiveness is. Forgiveness is a choice. It's a choice to obey God. The other person is not necessarily needed for forgiveness or reconciliation to take place between you and God. There are people no longer in my life I have apologized to God for the hurt I caused them because through situations or certain circumstances, I could no longer apologize to them personally. I have a friend, I'll call her Sue. Sue and her father had one of those estranged love-hate relationships and would get into loud shouting matches. She would lose control and scream to her father she wished he were dead. I would hear of this and say, "Don't say that! You really don't mean that." In her anger still she would say, "Oh yes I do!" Guess what happened? He died suddenly, not long after one of those screaming matches. He died of a heart attack one beautiful summer afternoon. Sue was physically and emotionally destroyed to the point she could not function.

As one might expect she blamed herself for her father's death, but the truth is he had many other heart attacks and the cause was his bad eating habits. Bearing the loss of a father is very painful; feeling you caused it is something entirely different. Now what does Sue do? How does she receive forgiveness? How can this situation be reconciled? Is all hope lost? She needs to get right with God and she needs healing. One day Sue cries out to God. She repents of her sins for not only what she said, but for not honoring her father. She is then released from her self-ordained prison.

Being right with God needs to override your hatred and bitterness for those that wronged you.

Being right with God needs to override your hatred and bitterness for those that wronged you. Don't let those that hurt you continue to hurt you by separating you from God and His wonderful blessing, presence and provision. I will be honest and straight- forward with you. I really don't care what people think of me as long as my God's happy with me. As long as I am in the clear and in the right with Him, I know everything is going to be alright.

So before we care about reconciling with others we need to be aware if *we* are in the wrong. Is God pleased with the attitude we have taken in offense of brother or sister so and so? Remember God can read our minds and hearts and weigh our true motives and intentions. Have *we* handled it the best we could? Paul says it like this in **Romans 12:17,** "If it is possible, as far as it *depends on you,* live at peace with everyone."(Author's emphasis)

In some cases we cannot reconcile to everyone. For example those who are deceased or will not under any circumstances listen to even the thought of reconciling back with us. Therefore, God wants us to obey His commands, and that is **"to forgive their sins or your heavenly father will not forgive you of your sins"** (Matthew 6:15).

That has nothing to do with the other party but everything to do with you and me personally. We make the first move. Don't ever wait on anyone else. It's our responsibility.

Before we move on to the next and greatest of all, the misconceptions about forgiving, I want to share with you a very important truth that will help you move into the blessing of forgiveness, and that truth is this: **You don't create forgiveness, you enter into it.** I know forgiveness is hard. Some cases seem down right unapproachable, or even impregnable. However you are not *making* forgiveness or having to plow the tough ground to plant forgiveness seeds for a later harvest. We don't make forgiveness, we enter into it. The blessing is already there and supplied for us through the commandment of God. For I have learned when He speaks to us and commands us to do something, He has already provided the way. He has made the way for us. He has the healing for our wounds; we just need to enter in to it. It's like salvation. He has provided salvation for us through the blood of His Son, His precious sacrifice, and all we have to do is accept it and believe it. The next step is to walk it out. We are to work out our own salvation (Phil 2:12).

Forgiving is the same way. We enter the door and walk out the path. Forgiveness then becomes a process by the way we become more and more perfect like our Heavenly Father is perfect. Loving our enemies and praying for those that spitefully use us. We choose to forgive because he forgives us. We choose to walk it out because of the mercy God shows us as we ourselves stumble along this rocky terrain of life. I choose to show mercy because of the mercy shown to me. I *know* of the unconditional love He has shown me. Therefore, I love.

Forgiveness is Not Forgetting

The biggest misconception in forgiving someone is thinking God is asking us to forget about the hurt that was caused us. **Forgive and forget** is a popular statement but not a biblical one. God is asking us to forgive, not forget. Forgiving someone is not forgetting what they did.

I once asked the man that was abused by his father his whole life, "Do you think you can ever forgive him?" His jaws tighten and his eyes were suddenly caught up in a deep hot flame; through clenched teeth came a voice rooted deep in years of hurt. He replied to me, "I can never forgive that son of a b@#*h. I can't forget it."

Ghost from The Past

The modern day war ship of steel was steaming along somewhere far in the Atlantic Ocean. Sometime around 2:30 am, I was laying on my back in my rack looking above at the pipes that run along its frame and listening to the ship's diesels humming its steady tune. My rack was next to the hull and I'm listening to the sound of the waves making its way alongside the ship with its calming whooshing noises. However, in my mind pops up my high school sweetheart and suddenly after all these years I get a close encounter in my mind with her ghost from the past. Her face is clear to me after all these years and the pain she always caused me is even clearer. How strange, I wasn't thinking of her but there she is. I began to relive all the hurt and situations she put me through. I relived all those memories one by one until I was in a mess. I was hurt and very angry all over again. I just came off watch and was trying to settle down but now I'm distraught. I can't believe someone could affect me so much after such a period of time. I wasn't living for Jesus at the time and I really didn't know what to do. But God was right there with me and I could feel His presence even though I wasn't living for Him. Some of the greatest times with God have been when I felt I didn't know Him personally or felt any way I needed Him.

I cried out to God and said these words, "I forgive her." The anger began to reside, and a great peace settled upon me and I dosed off to sweet peaceful sleep. Anytime her ghost thought she could just take a stroll through my mind and heart, I would say, "I forgave her." Over and over, each time she would appear. One day, I realized she was gone never to come back to harm or stick me with the blade of our past; and further more she took the hurt and pain with her! God took the pain from the wound, and the scar over my heart was completely healed! Glory be to

God! What great love and mercy the Father shows us!

Forgiving Doesn't Push the Erase Button in Our Minds.

Just because we forgive someone doesn't mean it is gone from our minds! Saying **"**I forgive you,**"** doesn't erase the memory of the time they hurt you. You will probably always remember it. But the pain isn't always going to be there. I kept forgiving my high school sweetheart until one day it honestly didn't affect me anymore. It was gone! We will look at these Biblical principles in a moment. But first here comes a big secret most people don't know. God is not asking you to forget it!

Forgiving is not forgetting. Forgiving is **not** saying to the offender, "It's okay what you did to me." No, it's **not okay**. Forgiving is not excusing what they did or sweeping it under the rug. Forgiving is not covering over what they did to you with your sacrifice of humbleness and forgiving attitude. Forgiving is not weakness or **accepting** what they did to you.

However, forgiving is acknowledging the hurt they caused you and choosing the right way to handle things over the wrong way to handle things. Forgiving is obedience to the Lord God. **Forgiving is understanding the love and forgiveness we are given!**
Forgiveness is a sweet smelling aroma in the nose of God. Forgiving is sometimes a trial or test. Forgiveness is a gift from God. Forgiving is releasing the most powerful forces

in the Universe to work on your behalf. Forgiveness is available to you and everyone at all times. But, forgiving is not forgetting.

Battle Scars

Let's take a look at the one man in history that was abused so badly at the hands of His enemies He was unrecognizable as a man (**Isaiah 52:14**). I'm speaking of course about Jesus. His close friends betrayed Him. He was beaten and spit upon, whipped to no end. His beard was even pulled out. He was falsely accused. He was laughed at and mocked. He was stripped naked and humiliated. They pushed a crown of thorns into His skull. They made him carry His own cross in which they intended to nail Him upon once he reached the top of the hill. They nailed Him to the tree by hammering nails through His wrists and feet. All His bones were showing and out of joint. This is just a few of the things they did to Him. The final thing they did was jab His side with a spear to see if He was dead or not. But before they did this and before He gave up His spirit to God, He forgave them. He said, *"Father, forgive them for they know not what they do!"* Now we know the end of the event. They took Him down and laid Him in a borrowed tomb. But three days later He rose! Praise God. But watch this. He then appears to His disciples after He arose, went to heaven and came back again. He shows the disciples His hands and feet while in the midst of where they were gathered together. Let's look at it in **John 20:26** and take it up where Jesus enters the room.

> "Peace to you!" Then He said to Thomas, "Reach your
> finger here, and look at my hands; and reach your hand
> here, and put it into My side. Do not be unbelieving, but
> believing."

Jesus was asking Thomas to put his hands in His scars so that Thomas would believe it was His Lord, the same one that was crucified, not a ghost. You see even though Jesus has forgiven them, He still remembers what they did, and has the scars to prove it. Even though we forgive those that hurt us, we will always have the scars to prove the past was real. The risen Jesus has the scars from those that hurt Him and still remembers even while in His glorious new body. The next text is my favorite concerning His scars. It's **Isaiah 49:15-16:**

"Can a woman forget her nursing child, and not have compassion on the son of her womb? Surely they may forget yet I will not forget you. See, I have inscribed you on the palms of My hands;"

Jesus not only remembers the punishment but He has the battle scars so He ***won't*** forget. The scars actually remind Him of us. Our own scars are battle wounds and can also act as reminders of the goodness and glory of our gracious Father! They serve as a living testimony to His love and mercy! Our scars could be a blessing. God will heal us from the pain and hurt and leave us a scar. He promises in

Exodus 20:24," *In every place where I record My name I will come to you, and I will bless you.*"

I look at the healed scars and smile while I remember. He comes to my mind and heart and blesses me. I remember where I've been and how far I have come. But most importantly I remember the mercy and goodness of the Lord. For He takes away all my pain and His mercy endures forever!

CHAPTER
5

OUR WOUNDS CAN SHAPE US.

D o you have a wound or does a wound have you? Like a knife that cuts the skin and leaves a scar to remember it by, make no mistake the hurts we have experienced will leave scars as well. The scars remind us of what we lived through and we will always have them; however, the wound itself can and must be healed. The problem is, a wound can mold or shape us without us really knowing it and can be the problem we are still dealing with today. Even worse, we can wrap ourselves around our wounds and they can become a blanket of security, reliving them over and over so we can have an excuse to back away or sulk in our current woes. But most of the time, we don't realize the pain that was caused to us is affecting our emotions and thought process now. Even worse still, that affects not only you but those around you.

Example Number One
The Pharisee's Camp

The year is 1980 and I am invited by a close friend to a summer camp in West Virginia. I'm around 9 years old and I remember looking at the red brochure that was handed to me. I was told it was a Christian camp and you could stay in huts by the lake where there was fishing and even softball fields for me to show off my talents as a strong hitter. Just bring your own glove. The age groups were broken down into groups and that's who you would be grouped with; boys my age would be my bunk mates. The oldest boys, thirteen year olds, had their own huts.

We were to be watched and supervised by an adult that was a hut leader and worked at the camp. I was so excited. I had a Peanuts book at home about camp and it sounded the same. Charlie Brown and Snoopy made it look fun. I almost expected Charlie Brown to be opposite of me in the canoe races we were going to have.

To grasp the understanding of what it is I'm about to tell you must keep in mind I'm around 9 years old and this will be my first trip away from home and the first time leaving mom and dad for 2 whole weeks; however, I felt I could handle it. But mainly the pull of adventure was too strong for the adventurous imagination of this dreamy blonde-headed boy. After all, it was a Christian camp so everything would be fine. I was going with a good friend of mine so we paired up and headed for "By God" West Virginia.

The route to the camp took us off the main road for a good distance as a dirt road snaked us through great wheat fields to where it opened up into ball fields and, beyond that, a small pond. I saw the huts along the edge of the bank of the pond and several of the boys that had already arrived trying out the fishing hole. I got out of the car, and after the goodbyes, my friend and I walk around to view where we would be spending the next two weeks of our lives. I remember walking to the pond first just to be around someone else to get a feel of what was going on. I wasn't really sure of where I was or what I was supposed to be doing.

Children were still arriving and till then, people were doing their own thing. As I approached the pond, I saw one of the adults standing at the pond, who (like everyone else) was someone I had never laid eyes upon. As he sees me coming, he shouts in my direction, "Hey who is that girl? Is that a girl? Hey we don't have hair like that around here." His shouts made it very clear he was offended and angry as he hurled his accusations in my direction. I looked around because I wasn't sure if he was talking to me; I was with other people. I felt confused. *Is he talking to me?* I thought. *What is he talking about?* I don't even know this guy. I'm a kid far away from home and don't know what I'm doing and this guy starts off with my first impressions by yelling at me. This is not good and I'm still not sure if he was talking to me. Finally I walk up to the pond's edge and stand looking at the water with the rest of the new arrivals and the accusation-throwing counselor is helping a boy tie his hook and still hurling his hate remarks in my direction. "Hey we don't have girls sleeping in our huts; the girls huts are over there. Oh, you're a boy I thought for sure you were a girl!" This guy keeps making remarks to me about my hair. I had no idea why. From what I could understand he thought somehow it was too long. This was 1980 and my hair was really blonde and I had a bowl-style haircut at the time which barely reached the back of my neck but it covered my ears. I didn't know why he was mad at me and I didn't know why my appearance was so offensive to him or anyone else for that matter.

I'm 9 years old and this is what was going through my heart and mind. **What have I done? Why is everyone mad at me for the way I look? Why am I not accepted for the way I look? Why is my appearance not acceptable to everyone? Why is God mad at me? Why doesn't God like me or my hair? What does my hair have to do with anything? Why doesn't God accept me the way I look?**

Little did I know that day would impact my life. I would carry those questions and scars around me for as many days as it took for me to lay them down at God's feet and allow Him to heal my heart and conscience.

My story of Camp "Religious pharisee training prison" is not through by a long shot. After the pond encounter I hear through the grapevine they are going to force me to cut my hair. I remember thinking, "how? I'm at camp. Who's going to cut my hair? Why?" I spent the next 2 weeks being threatened with having my hair cut. The fear was the worst part. It was not fun at camp; it was a nightmare. Charlie Brown was nowhere in sight and now that I think about it, that's probably why Ole' Charlie Brown or Linus didn't have any hair for kids their age-- this camp! I felt like I was at a boot camp and the rulers of the camp were arguing among themselves if they should cut my hair. It finally was decided, *"Yes. God wants it that way."* I suppose in their minds, God doesn't care for bowl-style hair cuts on 9 year old boys, and I was definitely a threat to everyone's survival as far as they were concerned.

This was 23 years ago and I remember it like it was 2 minutes ago. Even though they decided to cut my hair they didn't have anyone to cut it, and no one was volunteering; so they made my hut leader do it. While everyone else was out playing softball I was told to stay in the hut and this man set me on a stool in front of a mirror and kept apologizing over and over about what he was about to do. He told me they were making him do this, but he didn't want to. He said he had to because it was the rules of the camp. He then told me he had never cut hair a day in his life and didn't know how to do it now. He then proceeded to cut my hair off the best he could with a pair of scissors.

I don't remember anyone else getting a haircut that day or any other day. To my knowledge, no one else received a haircut that day and I was singled out because of the way I looked. The worst part of it all is this. No one ever told me **WHY**. Why are you doing this? Why is it a rule of the camp? What is wrong with the way I look? When the other kids saw me later on they asked, "What happened to you?" My hair was thinned to my scalp and all gapped up and uneven. When camp was over, I went home and I was at my friend's house waiting for my mom and dad to pick me up. I was in the corner of the living room playing an Atari game and they came in and went running by their own son, eagerly looking for me to wrap their arms around me to welcome me home. It was the first time they had ever let me go. They searched the whole house and came back into the living room and asked, "I thought you said Jason was here, where is he?" My friend's parents said, "He's right there!" They turned to see me sitting there, my hair gone. Their mouths dropped. They didn't even recognize their own son.

Things got worse because nobody did anything about it. They were outraged but they did nothing. No one made a phone call to those responsible, nothing. Worst still, they didn't sit me down and tell me **WHY** either, or that what those people did was wrong. They didn't let me know that what happened to me was not my fault. So guess what? I was lead to believe, not only those responsible for my haircut were in the right, but it was okay what they did. It was my fault my hair was cut like that. That is the message that was sent to my heart yet again. No one was looking out for me or stood up in my defense. It was all justified.

Some of you that have read this slice of my life might not grasp what happened. You might be thinking, *I don't get it, he got a bad haircut. What is the big deal?* Some of you probably read it with your heart breaking and some with your mouths open. Some of you with children probably imagined your child going through this and angrily thought what you would do to the guilty party. We're talking about how our wounds shape our life, so let me show you just how this window in time has affected my life until now. Though my wound took two weeks to shape me, it can take even less time to bend or warp your perception on daily life by just one word or small altercation.

Yesterday's Wound Not Dealt with is Today's Pain

It was Easter Morning 2004 a long way from 1980, and I was serving as an Associate Pastor in a very contemporary charismatic-style church. We preach Christ's resurrection often and celebrate it even more, and I was in the frame of mind of not wearing a traditional suit for anticipation of a great celebration service of freedom and rejoicing! So I wore my bright green Tommy Hilfiger dress shirt (no tie or coat) with black dress slacks and shoes. I thought I looked sharp; I was dressed up but yet relaxed enough to get down and really worship my risen Savior. When I got to church and walked into the sanctuary, my Pastor was just ending his "talk" to a few ushers who did not wear a tie and coat, and walked over to me with a stern look in his eyes and said, "Please tell me you brought a tie and coat!" I was shocked and said, "No sir, I didn't." He seemed to have a look of disgust with me and everyone else and then replied, "It's Easter and we have a lot of guests coming today and no one is even wearing a tie!" The strangest thing happened to me. It was as if the wind got knocked out of my sails. I thought, "What did I do? What's wrong with the way I was dressed? I thought I looked nice? What's wrong with me? Why is he mad at me? Why am I not dressed properly for God? Why am I not acceptable the way I am?

Do you see the pattern that has taken effect? Let me ask you, did you catch that? Does what I was thinking sound familiar? All of a sudden, I'm 9 years old again and it felt like someone had just stabbed me in the heart. I mean it really did a number on me. My mind went to another time and place and I went into a kind of dream state. I sat down in a chair stunned as everyone around me made preparations for the morning service. They sounded like Charlie Brown's teacher to me. Wah wah-wah- wah wah. I wasn't mad at what my Pastor said to me, or even blamed him, but I was literally crushed on the inside. I really felt exhausted and I didn't know why; though I'm a grown man, I felt like a little child.

I knew something was up and I had enough maturity and a close enough relationship with God to ask the Holy Spirit, "Hey what's up?" "What's wrong with me?" "Why am I feeling this way? Why did that affect me so much? What's the difference between the way he talked to me today and any other time?" That tone from him was usually par for the course, but something was wrong and I couldn't recover or snap out of it. Worse still, when it was time for service, I was still a thousand miles away and couldn't get into one of the greatest celebrations of all, the day we all celebrate our risen Lord. I just couldn't shake it.

I thank the Lord for my partner in life, and my special gift from God, my wife Karen. It just so happened I had told my camp story to her for the first time just a couple of days earlier. As we drove home from service, I told her what happened at church and how I couldn't shake it, I asked her, "Why did the wind get knocked out of me like that?" She replied, "Oh I know! Jason, it's the camp thing all over again!" *It's true, two are better than one and more powerful!* That's why we have spouses! The Holy Spirit rang on the inside of me "That's it! That's it!" I said, "You're right sweetheart! Thank you."

The Holy Spirit showed me I never dealt with that wound and I have been carrying that hurt and pain my whole life. When I got home I got on my knees in my prayer closet and poured my heart out to God. I thanked him for showing me this, and began to search myself and was so surprised something so long ago could be pulling my strings today. I laid it all down at His feet and boy did I feel better. I went through it all. I forgave all those at the camp, the man that cut my hair, my mom and dad for not doing anything and even my Pastor for how he spoke to me. Months later I got to have lunch with my Pastor and told him the story and He sincerely apologized and told me he didn't mean to hurt me. "Oh I know" I told him. He then said, "You know, Jason, sometimes God will purposely touch you on those spots to expose them." He was right and I knew God had touched me there so I could deal with it. I am better and stronger for it and more of the trash and dregs have been burned away in my life by the fire of God. I'm so much stronger on the inside than I was before, because God has done such a work in me. I want to give God the praise and let you know that I have been tested many times lately and put in situations where I could have easily been offended and I wasn't, my heart was quiet and at peace. On such times I walk away with a big grin and with my eyes closed, praising God for His goodness.

Example Number 2
No Ice Cream For You!

I can joke now because God healed me miraculously, but up until last year I had to be confronted with another wound. I think this is the biggest one of all and had the longest impact. I will make a long story short.

I was in the second grade and my teacher brought homemade ice cream for everyone in class. She really built up the suspense and anticipation of the treat and held it over our heads for ransom throughout the duration of the class. "Everyone be good and we'll have ice cream at the end." Nothing is better than home-made ice cream.

When I was that age I let my sense of humor get the best of me and regularly made smart remarks in class. My humor usually met the paddle around the corner at 2:00pm every day. However, to this day I can't remember what I said or did. I do know it was not major or worthy of the punishment. I had to sit in the corner, and was told I wouldn't get any ice cream. I sat there in the corner with my back to the class sulking in my punishment of banishment but keeping up hope that I could still have ice cream and she truly was joking and no ice cream was only a threat. At the end the ice cream was handed out, and guess what? No ice cream for me.

As the kids enjoyed their ice cream it got later and later and still the teacher would not relent. I remember thinking in my second grade little heart, **"You can keep your ice cream, I don't want it."** I remember hating the other kids as I thought *they were no better than me and how come they get ice cream?* Then the teacher did the strangest thing. She asked the other kids. "Class, do you think we should let Jason have some ice cream?" They all pronounced in one loud voice" "YEEESS!" No one said no and no one hesitated. I was shocked but do you know what? It was too late. My heart was bent. I felt betrayed. I was bitter and I really didn't want *the stinking ice cream.* The only way I could fight back was by throwing up a wall of **"I don't want what you have to give me."** It is a wall that would remain for 30 years, until I laid it down at the feet of Jesus. I took the cup of ice cream as others were finishing their cups and sat there slowly eating it and thinking deeply to myself. I felt wounded and saddened somehow, not rejoicing over any treat. I also felt like I was betraying myself for taking the ice cream. I bet you didn't know such strong feelings and trauma could occur in the heart of such a young child. Oh, but they can.

Healing The Wound

Last fall I was sharing this story in a counselor training session with my friend Tony. He could see it affected me still and he said in reference to the teacher, "Jason, can't you see that woman was crazy?" Does that sound like rational behavior to you? Would you govern your class room that way by letting the children have say over you?" I began to think of the other things I saw my teacher do. One time I saw her threaten a student by opening up a desk stapler so that it butterflies, and lift up the boy's shirt and press the stapler to his stomach and threaten to punch it if he didn't behave. I think that student had punched another student with the stapler and that was his punishment. I realized she *was* crazy. I also realized that I had been viewing that situation from my view point and that of a child all these years. Just like the hair cut incident, I was instantly a child again. Not until Tony suggested it and made me look at it now from the view of an adult, did I realize the damage that was caused. Tony's heart broke realizing I had been carrying that around for over 20 years. **How has that affected my life? well let's see.**

1. I'm at any party, "Would you like to dance?" **My Reply,** Always "No" *while thinking,*" Get away from me."
Translation. *I don't want what you are offering. Keep the ice cream*

2. Every body gets on the A- B honor roll at school. **My Reply,** "You can have your honors."
Translation. *I don't want to be recognized or singled out. I don't want to be a part of the rest of the group and what they are doing. Keep the ice cream.*

3. I'm in the Navy and just got promoted to Petty Officer 3rd Class, an E-4 in less than 2 years; everyone cheers, **My Reply,** I sneer and say "You can keep it, I wouldn't want to be Admiral of the fleet if you offered it to me, there's nothing you have I want."
Translation. *I refuse to accept what you have, I don't want what you have. I don't want your reward. Don't single me out or recognize me after all. Keep the ice cream.*

4. I refuse to use even coupons or get bonus deals. $25.00 off if you buy this. Or buy one get one free. **My Reply,** "Keep it." I don't need your favors.
Translation. *I don't want your free stuff or anything else you have to get me by doing me a favor in your eyes. Keep the ice cream.*

5. Hey Jason, let me take you to lunch today. **My Reply,** "Nope. Don't want what you have to give."

Translation. *I don't want or need anything from you. I don't want to give you any chance to hold something up over my head. So you can just keep it. Keep the ice cream.*

6. Hey if you work hard or earn a degree you can do this or that. **My Reply,** "Nope, I'm not going to jump through hoops for that, you, or anyone else. You can keep it."
Translation. *I don't feel I deserve the reward at the end. I really rather not even try. I don't want what you have to offer as a reward, if I "do this" "I get this." Keep the ice cream.*

7. I'm at the concert or ball game, hey they are giving out free shirts and everyone is getting one, do you want one? **My Reply,** "No, I don't want one."
Translation. *Anything you have, you can keep it to yourself. I don't want what you are handing out that everyone loves and wants, especially if it's free and everyone is getting one. Keep the ice cream.*

8. Even when I visit someone's house, Jason would you like something to drink? **My Reply,** Every time is, "No, I wouldn't care for one, thanks." Even if I did want one.
Translation. *No, I don't want any charity. I have made my life by denying everything or anything given to me so I can stay away from rejection and pain. I surely don't need you hanging things over my head or offering free things as a compensation. I don't want give anyone a chance to Lord anything over me, so. Keep the ice cream.*

Did You Notice What Was Going On?

Did you catch the pattern and what I was doing? Did you see how it affected my life? Denying what people were offering me and not participating was my way of dealing with rejection and I was putting up a wall so that I could not be affected. By denying what people were offering me I was protecting myself from hurt and in my mind, I was depriving them of the chance, honor and satisfaction of lording anything over me. In essence I was saying, "I don't want your ice cream", "You can shove your ice cream," but ice cream took the form of so many things. "You can keep your (*fill in the blank*), I don't want it."

Back to the counsel meeting, Tony asked me, "Jason you have been carrying this for how long, over twenty years!?" Then he said," It seems to me you have another issue. You need to forgive yourself for taking the ice cream. "You have been punishing yourself ever since for accepting the ice cream." Then he finally said, "Jason, it's not your fault, that woman was crazy!" It was time to lay it down, and I did. Wow was it awesome. I forgave the teacher, I forgave myself for taking that ice cream and I laid my burden and wound down at the foot of the cross of Jesus Christ. He took it. Now I'm FREE!

The Test

Not long after that, maybe a week or two later, I

walked in as a guest into a large local church. They give a welcoming package to all guests which included a coupon for a free cup of coffee in their coffee shop. "You also get to keep the nice ceramic mug it came in, as a treat from us to say thank you for coming in," the Pastor announced as he went through his daily announcements. In the past I wouldn't have thought twice about that. I would never have even looked at the coupon. I would have said in my heart. "Thanks, but no thanks, you can keep it." "I don't want your free anything."

But this time Glory be the praise of my Father! I said in my heart, "I will! That's my cup of coffee!" After the service I stood in line and received my reward. It was great and I never had a better cup in my life. I keep the mug today as a reminder. I sipped my drink and thanked God for His goodness and mercy.

It's Time to Lay It Down

My friend, I run into fellow believers all the time where I see this same behavior that was in my life affecting their life. It's time to let it go. It's time to lay it down. Sometimes we have lived so long with the wound we don't know what it's like without it. We believe the lie and what people have told us. We are not who *they* say we are, we are who **GOD** says we are! Sometimes we have shaped our personality around the lies and hurts people have caused us.

It reminds me of dog owners that mistreat their dogs early on as pups. They curse them, beat them, treat them like they are no good. You can spot these dogs when they are older. They are aggressive, man-haters or they are opposite in behavior, they cower away from you in fear, wanting to come near you to be loved and to accept what you offer them, but they are skittish and dart around always on the perimeter, not letting anyone come close. Like a dog that was beaten, teased, cursed at or starved we carry that into maturity. We find ourselves aggressive, mean junk yard dogs, or the opposite, fearing and not trusting when someone is sincere. We are going to end this chapter by laying down the wounds that the Holy Spirit has exposed in your heart while you read my personal accounts.

Maybe you didn't get denied ice cream or had your hair cut by religious zealots, maybe your hurt came from your father or some other family member and you have been lashing out ever since. I know class-mates and co-workers can be cruel. Maybe they wounded you or betrayed your trust and you feel you can never trust anyone again. I could write another whole chapter on how teachers alone throughout the years have wounded me tremendously. The people we trust to love, teach or protect us are the ones that wound us the most. We will never get used to it. Because the greater the trust, the deeper the wound.

God has promised us, if we will draw near to

Him, He will draw near to us. Don't be afraid and be like that wounded dog that won't come near anyone, always longing for acceptance but incapable of trusting. Trust God. Whatever the Holy Spirit has brought up inside you as you read my personal accounts, let's give it to Jesus so He can begin to heal us. I want you to fill in the blanks with the proper names and situations. Let's pray:

Jesus,

*I thank you for bringing to my attention the wounds that shaped my life. I now realize how they affected me. I have been carrying them too long and I give all my wounds to you. I have believed what they said about me to be true. Thank you for perfecting that which concerns me personally and I believe what **you** say about me and I am who **you** say I am. I'm a child of the King.*

*Jesus, I forgive **Name(s)** for what they **Did or Said** to me. I lay it down at the foot of the cross and I ask you to start healing me of the wounds and start showing me the Truth from this day forward. Please correct any of my behavior that was a cause of those wounds. Thank you so much for touching me on that wound(s) so I could understand I had one and you want me healed. I release all the pain and hurt to you in your mighty name. Amen*

CHAPTER

6

LEARNING TO PROCESS

There is a saying, I'm not sure where it came from but, it is this: *Give a man a fish and you feed him for a day; teach him how to fish and you feed him for a lifetime.* We have just learned how our wounds affect us and how to lay them down, but now we need to learn how to process our future wounds and hurts. Believe me, they *will* come. I want to share three easy steps with you the Holy Spirit taught me that has worked for me and that can help you through a healthy cycle of processing future wounds situation.

First Step

You need to realize there is a problem. Have you ever been watching a movie and something on the inside of you ties you up in knots? Maybe it is a scene that doesn't affect anyone but you. As others continue to watch the movie with blank faces, you are sitting there with tears flowing down your face. You even think to yourself, "Why am I crying at this part?" "What in the world is wrong with me?" And you say to yourself, "this is not even a sad scene!" Well, you need to learn to say this to yourself,

"Okay, what's going on underneath the hood?" Let's look at it in terms of a car.

Just like us, a car is made up of many parts to keep it running smooth. When your tire makes that thump, thump, thump sound, your tire is flat and has taken a wound it could no longer conceal. The puncture affected the tire and it is letting you know. It could be a drastic wound such as a very large and sharp object that shatters the tire on impact. It could have been punctured lightly and over time letting out the air without you realizing it. Soon it has manifested itself into a physical symptom or problem. A physical symptom for example, would be the noises and sounds that come from the tire. The car is not able to continue and you are on the sidelines not able to reach your destination. It must be dealt with. In some cases even before you continue.

Or try this one, your battery could be dead so your car won't start, your carburetor could be clogged, so your car won't get gas. Your head light may be busted, and you can't see in the dark to make your destination. If we are crying in strange places or lashing out at others inappropriately we need to stop what we are doing and check underneath the hood.

Some common symptoms might include:

1. Lashing out at others.

2. Crying in unusual situations or places.

3. Anger.

4. Critical of others and their actions.

5. Feeling tired all the time.

6. Little things becoming difficult.

7. Avoiding certain people.

These are just a few. You will notice yourself or someone else might point something out. "Jason, I noticed you have been feeling and looking run down lately." Remember we affect those around us. You might not have caught on that you're really upset at John for getting that job in your place but your fake smile or avoidance of him altogether speaks volumes. Thump, Thump, Thump.

Second Step

Learn and remember to ask the Holy Spirit, "**Okay Lord, what is it about "this" that is affecting me so much?**" He may show you right then, or He may take His time to draw some other things to your attention; either way He will show you. Remember, I got an answer right away when I asked God about why I felt that way about my appearance, but the answer came through my wife. "I know why you feel that way!"

When I get mad I have learned to ask myself, **"Okay, what am I really mad at?"** I have learned it was never about the situation I thought got me mad. It was really more deeply rooted in my past. This can better be illustrated by an iceberg. You see the tip or a quarter of it sticking out of the water (this is the manifestation of us getting angry and yelling), the rest of the iceberg is what you can't see underneath the water line. It's what is really going on. Just for an example, you might tell your spouse everyday to pick up his clothes off the floor and one day you let him have it when he doesn't. You *think* you are mad because those undies on the floor broke you, but really, if you stop and ask yourself *what is really going on*, or **"What am I really mad at?",** you might feel that deep down inside no one takes you seriously or listens to what you say. You really start to think about this and trace it back all the way to fourth grade when "this or that happened", because, quite truthfully, yelling at someone for not picking up their clothes off the floor is not a *crisis* type of situation. It really is not a *yelling* type of situation.

Most of the time I could trace my anger back to my past, maybe even to kindergarten. Or, there is another solution. It just could be you have had a frustrating day and seeing those clothes on the floor for the hundredth time just broke you. We make poor decisions when we get tired.

There could be a Holy Spirit revelation surprise, you could find out that you have a perfectionism problem that was caused or implanted into you a long time ago! And, you thought you were just mad because of some clothes on the floor! I have learned when I ask God, "What am I really mad at?" I never know what He is going to show me or tell me. Remember to keep an open mind and like Mary said to Jesus' disciples, "What ever He tells you to do, do it!" (John 2:5)

Once we have identified the problem we need to learn that the only way we will get healed is through Christ. Don't be full of pride or naive to think you can handle the problem on your own. You can already see how well that has worked for you. Admit you need help so you can receive the healing.

Third Step
Your Healing is Following You!

God will give you healing if you humble yourself and ask for it; but He will let you go on hurting if you think you don't need help, refuse help or try to handle the situation on your own.

As with any situation I have shown you in this entire book, if you don't admit you need help then your healing and blessing is following you around everywhere you go. **Your breakthrough is waiting for you to stop and acknowledge there is something that needs to be broken through!**

So now you have asked yourself, "What am I really mad about?" The Holy Spirit has revealed something to you. You have traced the hurt or wound to the source. The third step is, **"Lay it down and give it over to Jesus."** Jesus said in Matthew 11:28:

Come to *me*, all you who are weary and *burdened*, and I will give you rest. Take *my* yoke upon you and learn from me, for I am gentle and humble in heart, and you will find rest for your

souls. For *my* yoke is easy and my burden is light."
(Author's emphasis added)

I want to show you something from His teaching.
First, notice He *invites* us and says come to Him. Who? All
those who are weary and burdened. If something has
manifested itself to you and it is affecting you, that "you"
is you! You are the "You" in that verse. Read it again and
see the word "you" in it. In just 3 lines He uses the word
5 times. If you are burdened with unforgiveness, that is
a burden. The second thing I want to show you about
this verse, one that ministers really miss a lot but it is so
important, is whose yoke are we carrying and whose yoke
does Jesus tell us to put on? I have emphasized them in
italics above. It's **His** yoke. We are carrying the wrong yoke
and one we shouldn't be carrying, period. So he invites us
to lay down our yoke and pick His up.

But here's what every one seems to miss. He is not
taking His yoke off and putting His yoke on you. He is
still carrying the yoke but inviting you and me underneath
His yoke! Jesus is the one that is still carrying His yoke. He
pulls the burden and load for us and we learn from Him!
Praise God for rest. How great is His love towards us! God
Himself is inviting us to lay it down. Do it!

Now, you have asked the Holy Spirit the problem
and He showed you the cause, and you are going to lay it
down to God. How do I go about doing that? To give God
the problem you need to gather all the players or factors in
the situation that hurt you. You need to include and forgive

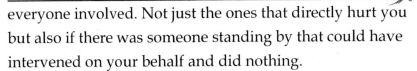

everyone involved. Not just the ones that directly hurt you but also if there was someone standing by that could have intervened on your behalf and did nothing.

For example, if you were physically abused as a child, as the Holy Spirit brought that hurt to light, your memory might include all those times another family member stood by and did nothing to intervene. Maybe it was a mother, or sibling. They ran and hid, afraid for their own safety. They looked the other way and pretended not to hear you or see you. That affects you now and you realize that resentment is the root of your own inability to trust or love them even until today. You just don't need to forgive the one that was physically abusing you; you might need to forgive all those around you who did nothing. I have some news for you. Doing nothing is just as big a sin as committing one.

So, when laying down our burdens to Jesus, we need to confess and bring to light everyone involved. Be honest. If there is just a little thing in the back of your heart or mind, don't hold on to it. Maybe you're asking, "Jason, how do I know if I got everybody?" Trust the Holy Spirit when you ask Him to reveal everyone to you. Ask Him that question. *"Holy Spirit is there anyone that I have resentment towards that I'm not aware of?"* Get quiet and listen with your heart. Don't be in a rush, wait on Him. Usually someone will pop up in your mind or in your vision of what happened. He might bring someone to mind, He might not. If you can't think of anyone and your heart and mind are quiet, then now you can lay it down including everyone involved. That's part of the process of forgiving, including everyone involved.

Now it's time to pray. Don't forget when you lay it down don't pick it up again. At the end, I will take you through a guideline for prayer, so you can learn to create your own prayer from your heart. When praying, thank Jesus for the knowledge He has given you and bringing it to your attention. Acknowledge the hurt and *all* those involved. Tell Him how it made you feel. Be honest. Say, I forgive _(the person's name)_ for what they did or did not do. Don't forget to include each person involved. Acknowledge to Jesus, *I lay down the yoke of bondage and I pick up your yoke to learn from you. Please take the hurt and pain and heal me.*

To close this chapter I will review the steps and enforce them in case they became blurry or lost. I put the main questions and steps in bold type and a reminder of what it is and how to process it underneath in italics.

We have:
Identified there is a problem and admitted we need to deal with it.
Now we:
Ask ourselves,

1. Okay what's going on underneath the hood?
Or Why am I acting this way? (thump thump)
2. What am I really upset (*mad*) about?

Or Why am I really acting this way? What's underneath it? (Iceberg)

3. Lay it down and all involved to Jesus.

Pray and don't pick it up again. Let Jesus have it. (His yoke)

Now all that is left is to walk it out. Forgiveness is a process. These three steps should help you have a good start down the road of processing the hurts or problems that come along. They have helped me time and time again. We must first learn to stop and look at ourselves first (plank in our own eye) before we react and look at the speck in other's eyes. If you need to, go back and review them.

CHAPTER
7

SEVENTY TIMES SEVEN

In the last chapter we looked at what forgiveness is and what it isn't. That's not the last word or a complete picture of what forgiveness means to God. That's only the start. As we walk out our forgiveness, God will show us new things and better ways of handling each situation. God does not have a blanket prayer or a one-size-fits-all way of covering things for every situation by any means; however, what I have shown you so far are basic kingdom principles to put us in the right direction and lay a good foundation.

In the last chapter, I shared with you a personal story about me lying in my bed and remembering the hurts and wounds from the past. Without even knowing how to handle it, I felt the Holy Spirit prompt me to say the words, "I forgive her." Then when the memory would arise and the potential was there to relive the past and get angry I learned to say, "I forgave her."

Little did I know that when I said those words, "I forgive her," I walked straight into a biblical principle and what the Word of God says about forgiving. Then every time she would come to mind and I professed in faith, "I forgave her," I was walking out the forgiveness.   Now I must point this out before we go on. I did that without knowing what scripture I was referring to. I didn't know from the scriptures that I was living out Matthew 18:22. The Holy Spirit is our counselor and our personal guide. He leads us and guides us to all truth. He teaches us in the way we should go. If the Holy Spirit speaks to your heart, listen and obey.

 Now let's look at our main scripture. Let's start with Matt 18:21:

> 21. Then Peter came to Jesus and asked, "Lord how many times shall I forgive my brother when he sins against me? Up to seven times?
> 22. Jesus said to him, "I do not say to you, up to seven times, but up to seventy times seven." (NKJV)

Forgiving someone that has hurt us and giving our wound and hurt to God **does not** push the *erase memory* button in our minds. Of course the memory will come up again. Memories are powerful and can bring the emotions that come with them. If you live them over again in your mind you can get hurt all over again. We will go over that before the end of this chapter, but first let's go back to the verse above.

You have no doubt heard by now that in this scripture we just looked at Peter was trying to be Mr. Spiritual and take the Jewish custom of forgiving their brother three times and doubling it six, then adding one more for goodness sake for the grand total of seven times.

Fine, I can see that and that does fit with the behavior pattern of Peter; however, Jesus shocks them by saying not up to seven times but seventy times seven!

Seventy times seven is 490! Is that 490 times in a minute, day, hour, month, life time? There's a reason He didn't specify. Actually this is a bigger type and shadow of the number 7 which means spiritual perfection and the number of Jerusalem which is 70 *Study the book of Daniel.* Seventy times seven is 490. What Jesus is trying to show us here is there's going to be a large amount of trial and error, growing and learning in your forgiveness with your brother. In other words it's a process over time! Jesus is saying, "You are going to have to forgive the way I forgive you Peter, or (*fill in your name here*), over and over and beyond, showing *undeserved* mercy to each other like I have for you!" Aren't you glad Jesus doesn't limit **His** forgiveness? Okay, Jason, that's seven times! You're out of here! I'm sorry you just don't make it.

No, true love is unconditional, always patient, always kind. We must show mercy to each other. We must show mercy like God shows us mercy. Don't you want mercy for yourself? Then show mercy. We are never any more like Jesus as when we show mercy! What Jesus is telling Peter is there is no limit to forgiving. Forgive them. They sinned against you again? Forgive them again. How many times? As many as it takes. Why? Because I forgive *you* that way, again and again. **We must understand the forgiveness that has been given to us.**

So that tells us that forgiving is not a number, it's an understanding from our heart. Our heart needs to be right. You can forgive a thousand times with your lips, and your heart not be right. But forgive once from your heart and you remove a thousand wounds. You can forgive once from your heart and gain the favor and ear of the Almighty God!

Forgiveness is an attitude of the heart! So, if you have forgiven them and given the hurt to God already, **every time that memory pops back into your head, as soon as it does, forgive them**! Don't relive it over again! Say to yourself or even out loud, "I forgave them!" Speak it in faith if you don't have it in your heart yet. I can promise you this, you won't make it to seven times seventy, before God does such a healing in your heart. I don't care if all you have is faith. Forgiveness is not a feeling! Speak it out, "Lord, I forgave him", "Lord, I forgave her" as many times as it takes.

One day you will look around and realize you have risen above the situation by the mercy and grace of God and the hurt will be gone. You will look around and not see those that hurt and accuse you, who seek to throw the stones of accusations, and the memories that wounded you will wound you no more. You will find yourself at the feet of Jesus who doesn't accuse you and He alone will tell you, "Go, You are free!"

What Do I Do When They Are Taking Advantage of Me?

You're probably saying right now, "Okay Jason, that process is for the memories of people that are not around me. What do I do when they are in my life right now and they are taking advantage of me?" I'm so glad you asked that! That is another big problem Christians face everyday because they don't know when they are doing the right thing. They are afraid of doing wrong and being outside the will of God. They think letting someone walk on them time and time again is the will of God for their lives. They don't know when they should tell a brother or sister they will no longer support them financially until they get a budget or get a job to support themselves.

Let's look at **Matthew 5:38-42.** Jesus is teaching us how to respond to those very people.

38: You have heard it said, "Eye for eye, and tooth for tooth," But I tell you, Do not resist an evil person. If someone strikes you on the right cheek, turn to him the other also. And if someone wants to take your tunic, let him have your cloak as well. If someone forces you to go one mile, go with him two miles. Give to the one who asks you, and do not turn away from the one who wants to borrow from you."

The first thing I want you to see is this. How many cheeks did Jesus tell us to turn? How many tunics did He ask to give? How many miles did He ask us to go beyond in these cases? In each case just one more. Our problem is we go three, four, five, six, seven, eight, nine, ten.... there has to be a stopping point. Does that mean I just go the extra mile once and stop? No, the willingness to give to those that ask things of us is not found in any number but the right attitude from the heart of giving.

Jesus is not teaching us a number in His teaching; He's teaching us the proper attitude and understanding about the kingdom. Jesus is teaching us about *His* way of doing things, and about *His* giving and love. But just because we should have patience and be gentle, kind and show mercy doesn't mean we should let people take advantage of us all the day long. As Christians we are not wimpy, pushovers or easy targets! We must be wise as serpents but harmless as doves. We need to use wisdom! Every case is different but every case involves using judgment and wisdom.

Does That Mean I Just Give Them One Chance?

All you have to do is get in one of these situations where someone is using you. You may already know what I'm talking about or you may not. If you don't, look out, this test is on the way. You keep giving and giving, turning your cheeks to be struck again and again. Soon or later you are going to fall to your knees and ask God, "when is enough enough?" I feel everyone should and will experience that situation sometime; maybe you are right now. There are some things you need to know.

First thing, yes, when someone asks to borrow

something, give it to them but use wisdom. If you only have one car to get to work and they ask to borrow your car for themselves, work something out. If ever you have it in your means to help someone do it. *In your means*, means, you have something you can give and help someone else with. **God blesses us so we can bless others!** You have a car you don't use, they need one. You have an extra bedroom and they need a bed. You have food to feed your family, they don't, give or buy them groceries for the week to help them out.

If it's in your means to do so, give. However they should always show improvement and be willing to help themselves.

Why should I give to them that asked to borrow? Because we understand we are all just stewards of everything we so call *own* anyway. It's all just *stuff.* People think God is trying to take away their *stuff.* God doesn't want your *stuff,* He doesn't need your *stuff.* He can bless you with better *stuff.* If you won't let someone borrow your *stuff,* your heart is in the wrong place and attached to the wrong *stuff.* There's that right attitude of the heart again.

Second, it's more than okay to help them financially but you better weigh and know each situation while using wisdom and sound judgment. I've known pastors to help members of their flock financially such as help pay back rent because a member comes to them with tears in their eyes and a tragic "we're behind" story. Meanwhile those same people haven't done one thing to help themselves.

No budget, no change in their way of spending. You go over their house to check on them and see all the DVDs, play station games and toys in front of the biggest plasma screen television you have ever seen in your life.

Your jaw drops to the floor and you hear one of their cell phones ringing and they tell you hold on a second, and put out their cigarette to answer the phone. They don't have rent money or can't pay the utility bill but they can buy cigarettes and the new X-Box game. You see why they were behind in their payments.

Next month they come to you again. "Hey could you help me out?" The light bill is due and the rent is coming up." Knowing now they brought those financial needs upon themselves we respond this way. "What steps have you taken to get out of debt and get your finances on track? Do you have a budget yet?" They say, "no, not yet." "Why don't you cut cable, lay off some of the entertainment, and possibly take back that television for a smaller one?" "Oh, I can't do that!" "Then neither can I help you until you help yourself!"

If they come to you again, should we turn them away if they come back needing help after they have truly helped themselves? Of course not. Each case is different, each case needs prayer and discernment. We are told to pray for those that spitefully use us. Now, the next couple that comes to you might legitimately need help financially and we should weigh the situation and do what is in our means. Give to those that ask of us.

Don't Relive That Painful Situation!

Take it from someone that knows from experience. I have a great deal of experience, at least fourteen years of reliving the painful past. I suffered greatly from depression, and if there is one thing I learned from it it's **"Do not relive those painful situations!"** When the memory pops in your mind that doesn't mean you entertain it and relive it. The thoughts will then own you and take you where they want you to go! You will relive the hurt and pain all over again. The first assault on us as believers is in our mind.

Our very first and most important commandment is "Love the Lord your God with all your heart and with all your soul and with all your **mind**" (Matthew 22:37). I have learned that if you think a certain way, even though your heart hasn't bought into it, soon your way of thinking will spill over into your heart. "For as he thinks in his heart, so is he" (Proverbs 23:7). This proverb tells of a man that is a *miser* and an evil man. He thinks a certain way but more importantly his heart believes the things his mind conceives. It all starts with the mind. We are assaulted all day in our mind by what we touch, hear, see and smell. That is the entry way into our temple. Our heart is the most important thing about us but it all starts with the mind. If our enemy can get you to think you're no good, and you entertain that lie and don't deal with him, then one day he will wear down your defenses and you will say to yourself, "I am no good!" Your heart just bought a lie. Then you live what is in your heart. In other words, what we take in our mind has a great influence on our heart, and our heart is our true self. God speaks to our hearts not our minds.

Resist Him

One day I was driving to a football game in Chapel Hill to watch the Tar Heels on a beautiful fall evening. I had the radio blasting and was looking forward to driving out of my troubles by putting them in the rear view mirror and heading towards something I enjoyed-- college football. I was alone that time in my life and I was really medicating myself with my pleasures and I had the radio louder than usual to drown out my thoughts or chase them away. Suddenly I heard the Holy Spirit break through my deception of enjoyment and I heard Him plainly say, "Turn the radio off for a second, I need to talk to you." I ignored him. I was angry and I didn't want to talk to anyone. He said it again. "Turn the radio off for a second I need to talk to you." I ignored Him a second time and there was silence. I got to the football game and sat there not really enjoying it. I was surprised to find that the last thing I had left that would for sure bring me pleasure did not. I went home discouraged, and worse off than before I came. I felt hopeless. Now I no longer cared for football.

I was driving back home in silence, the radio was now off and I began to relive all the things that happened to me in life. I remembered the hateful words and the holes I found myself in. This time it wasn't the Holy Spirit talking to me it was my enemy. Letting me lie to myself and telling me I was no good. No one wanted me, no one cares. No one wanted to come to the game with you, call you, come over or spend time with you, email you back or even share their life with you. In silence, I sat there with a frown listening to lie after lie, reliving the hurt and having my own little pity party. Then I bought it. Normally I would shake or excuse those thoughts but this time I held on to it and it took root. I then believed it in my heart. I swallowed those lies hook, line and sinker. *I am* no good! I then agreed and said it in my heart, "*Everyone is right, I am no good.* From this day forward I'm not going to care. I don't care about me, I don't care about you or life. If no one cares about me I'm going to give it back to them," was my thoughts, and then the obvious thought happened, "I wish I was never born. I just want to die. I just can't make it. They were right about me. I'm no good."

The next day at church I sat there on the front row on the far left side as usual. I am there for security for the Pastor, or as a personal assistant. If he ever needs anything, he looks my way. Nothing had changed in my attitude. I sat there not praising God or worshiping. I sat there with a distant blank look on my face. No one noticed, no one cared. I didn't care.

Then suddenly the strangest thing happened while the Pastor began to preach. He came down off the stage and walked down to the alter area and looked out over the audience. He then stopped as if someone stopped him in his tracks and he suddenly turned his head to me in a sudden quick look. He pointed straight at me and said, "Get up!" I was in shock. It was the middle of the service and this just happened. Everyone else was in shock and didn't know what was going on. He was talking to me like a father would sternly talk to his children to set them straight. His finger went from pointing at me to pointing down to his feet. "Get up and come here!"

I got up with my heart still sunk down deep in my chest. I was in a funk I have never been before and my heart was convinced I was no good. I wasn't just feeling sorry for myself, or trying to get attention. I really was convinced I was no good to myself or anybody. I arrived in front of the Pastor with about 800 people staring at us. I didn't care. Pastor Ken looked me in the eyes as the Holy Spirit fell upon him and had a word for me right on the spot. He spoke in "a thus saith the Lord" voice and pointed to me in my chest. "You are under warfare and the enemy has told you you are no good and nobody loves you or cares for you! He's said you are no good to yourself and no one else and you have believed that! But the Lord is telling you, you are My son!! And from this day forward I will show you who you are! You will never doubt again who you are. You are *My* son and I love you!" WOW!!!

You talk about lightning trapped in a bottle! I stood there with the Holy Spirit softening my heart as he spoke and then God zapped me a good one! I was shaking so bad I went back to the front row and sat back down as God was working on me from the inside. My Daddy God showed up, and in a second, did away with all the damage the devil had been doing to me for years! I felt my hands shaking and all I could do was cry. The preacher went back to preaching whatever he was talking about and then suddenly I felt two hands wrap around my shoulder as I felt a friend of mine, Carl Ham, come over to love on me. "I love you buddy," he said, he even cried a little with me. It must have been the anointing making him cry because it was that powerful lightning and electricity feeling that didn't leave me for several days. From that day forward, I never bought the enemy's lies and I began to learn who I was in Christ. I have never been the same since! Glory be to God! God's touch and understanding of His love itself fed me alone those next several days. Everyone around me was shocked. No one would have guessed I thought those things about me, many came up and hugged me and told me how much I meant to them. I want to let you know before we move on. You never know what that person on your left and right is going through when you come to church on Sunday, don't let the outer appearances fool you. We need each other. It still amazes me to this day the love God has for me that He would stop what was going on in a service and point me out. How great is Your Love oh Lord!

That all started with me entertaining the thoughts

that popped in my mind. **Do not relive those past hurts and wounds!** The truth is, we relive them so we can get comfort from those little pity parties we have. If you're not careful, you can get addicted to them. That is a false comfort and never healthy or good for you. Before we end I want to share with you what to do when those thoughts do pop in your mind. You are in control of your mind. Believe me, you can't control what pops in there, but you can control what happens when they do! Listen to the way Paul writes about the warfare in II Corinthians 10:3:

> For though we walk in the flesh, we do not war according to the flesh. For the weapons of our warfare are not carnal but mighty in God for pulling down strongholds, casting down arguments and every high thing that exalts itself against the knowledge of God, *bringing every thought into captivity* to the obedience of Christ. (NKJV author's emphasis.)

That's what we have to do! Bring every thought into obedience with Christ! Put those hurts under the obedience of Christ. I want to give you two illustrations that I use. I have used them so much I don't remember where they came from or I would give them credit. First you already know what to do when you get those memories of the people you have already forgiven. "I forgave him, or her" Another illustration is I want you to picture a pond with the bad thoughts as turtles. When one raises its head you pop him on the head with a gun. I heard this works for some people. The one I use is this. When something pops into my mind that does not belong there or doesn't fit who I am in Christ or exalts itself against God, I say, "That does not fit who I am, get out of there!" Normally it does, you can limit these things by what you listen to and watch on television or the big screen. We shouldn't use our minds for the devil's trash can. If it doesn't go away or if that certain thought you know is against God tries to come again, I usually say, "Get behind me Satan; you are not mindful of the things of God, only man!" That has worked for me every time. One last thing, being depressed is a choice. We choose to be depressed. They taught me that in seminary and I have found from experience it is true. I no longer wallow in self-pity, or relive past hurts in my mind. I choose the way of the Lord, I know who I am, and I have the mind of Christ. I will end with 1 Peter 5:8 as a reminder to both you and I:

> Be sober, be vigilant; because your adversary the devil walks about like a roaring lion, seeking whom he may devour. **Resist him**, steadfast in the faith, knowing that the same sufferings are experienced by your brotherhood in the world." (NKJV author's emphasis.)

PART THREE

RECEIVING FORGIVENESS

The Spirit of the Lord is upon Me,
because He has anointed Me to preach the gospel
to the poor. He has sent Me to heal the brokenhearted.

~ Jesus Christ (Luke 4:18)

CHAPTER

8

I'M MAD AT GOD!

f I stood in front of two thousand people and asked, "I want to see a show of hands of all the people who have ever been mad at God or feel God has hurt you," and if everyone were honest with themselves, I bet two thousand hands would go up and the first one up would be my own. So, what do you do when the person you feel wounded you the deepest is God himself? How do you forgive the God of all creation? What do you do when you are mad at God?

Will You Trust Me or Walk Away?

Several years ago my sister-in-law Lisa was diagnosed with breast cancer. She was a woman of God, 40 year old, mother of two and a working wife, and trusted God with all her heart. Well, my entire family is a family whose faith and trust is in God, so immediately we began to pray and believe God for her healing. What amazed me were the people that came out of the woodwork into the fight. It seemed a line was drawn in the sand. All those believing in God, *The* God over cancer and our healer, step over here. All those immediately pointing a finger and saying, "You are going to die; you have cancer and there is no help for you," over on that side. Did that happen? Did people actually point and say, "Ah ha, now you are in for it, you faith-church people, let's see your God save you now" in a time of great need? You can bet your life they did. Some were so-called close friends and family.

You can believe me when I say that this tested my forgiveness level and maturity in my walk with Christ. I found my jaws clenched tight on a number of occasions. Don't get me wrong, we were bombarded with love and affection and support from most family and friends and our fellow Christians that stepped up and supported us from day one and stayed in the fight. I had complete confidence in my Lord as I always do. However, things grew worse and more bad news would come. What was strange was good news would be mixed in with the bad and we could see God was with us through the fight.

However bad news became the usual report and only seemed to get worse. At first I shrugged it off and kept believing "we don't go by sight" and all that. "Whose report will you believe?" and all that. We went through a ton of healing scriptures and scriptures on hope and God's promises. There was not one day that went by in which we didn't pray. One time our Pastor called for a church fast and I personally fasted for 3 days. We all took this very seriously and many others joined in to add their faith to ours and continually lift Lisa up in prayer. We believed with all our might and heart Lisa would recover.

We had an auction for her and raised 10,000 dollars for her treatments. Lisa was loved by everyone, and it was safe to say you couldn't find anyone to say a mean word about her. To her, everyone was "baby doll;" when she saw you she would say, "Hey, baby doll!"

Things grew even worse and as I heard bad news I would shut the door to my prayer closet and tell God we trusted him, but I would ask, "What is going on?" Each prayer time I could hear my own frustration as my voice would get louder and louder. However, I still trusted Him fully. Then more bad news would come. Cancer spread to her brain and all over her body. Soon she would have trouble walking as her legs would not respond to her will. I found myself in my prayer closet losing control and yelling at God shaking my fist. " You are the Healer and our God!" "Why haven't you healed her? " Are you not bigger and stronger than cancer? You are making our enemies laugh at us and you are proving them right! They laugh and say she has cancer, church stuff is one thing but this is real world stuff, she has cancer and she is going to die and you are proving them right! Aren't you bigger than cancer? Am I supposed to believe in you as God Almighty, but just don't get cancer, because God is not bigger and stronger than cancer? Cancer kicks your butt all over the place!" I actually screamed those things out loud, I was so frustrated.

Always remember this when you pray, God welcomes your honest prayers. You will actually get more accomplished when you get right up front and pour your heart out; He knows what we are really thinking anyway. Be honest with God. He welcomes your honesty, however, anytime I yelled and fussed, I always apologized to Him and thanked Him for letting me vent out my frustrations and for always being there. After all He is The Sovereign Lord and is to be feared, respected and honored; yet He is big enough to handle my immaturity and remembers we are made from the dust.

The Rubber Meets the Road

This test with my sister-in-law is where the rubber meets the road. Because she was a child and servant of God and walked in His ways and she got cancer, what about the rest of us? I would ask God, am I next? Could I get cancer? Would you do that to me? Am I not protected? I always have felt "safe from harm" because I stay under His wing. We were all about to get our questions answered. Does God allow bad things to happen to His children? Are we protected? I will share with you the answers to these questions in the last part of this chapter, but first I must tell you what happened in the case of my sister-in-law.

The situation became worse and her health left her, soon she would enter the hospital for the final time. Family and friends were gathered around Lisa's bed singing and praising God when suddenly a strong sense of peace literally fell in the room and settled on each person, then the Spirit of the Lord took my sister-in-law and the battle was over. I know that it was *He* that took her because of the peace that transformed our hearts at the time, *always remember the devil can never duplicate real and lasting peace; He just counterfeits it through temporary things of the world.*

I was not there at that time, I was home praying and crying out and literally travailing to God like I never have in my entire life. I felt so helpless and cried out with all that was in me. That same peace that entered the room at the hospital entered my dwelling and consumed my heart. Peace fell upon me and I knew everything would be alright.

Lisa was so well loved that the night of the wake there was a 3 hour wait just to come by and meet the family. The workers at the funeral home said in all their years they had never seen anything like that and also they said, "We never got to meet this woman, but we sure wished we had!"

My friend, we all have gotten mad at God one time or another, and we feel the reasons are legitimate, but I have found most of our trouble and pain come from our own ignorance in the knowledge of God. God's ways are not our ways and we will get along better when we come to the knowledge of His ways of doing things. Now, if we experience a great loss, the pain we feel is real and serious, it's just misdirected in a **lack of understanding** when we direct our anger from the pain towards God. I have found that we get mad at God because something didn't come out the way *we* wanted or *we* didn't get *our* way in that particular situation. We feel God let us down or didn't live up to the way *we* thought He should. In essence, we are trying to play God's role and do God's job. I have a friend that says, "The greatest day in my life was the day I found out there really is a God, and it ain't me." I want to share with you some true lessons I have learned to help you in this situation.

The Fall of Man

We are first going to where it all began, to the source. God created man to be with Him and they walked together in unity until man sinned against God by doing opposite of His commands and his sin separated him from God. When that happened we became outcast from His presence and we began to die. When we became separated from God, not only did we begin to die spiritually, but our bodies began to age and die. To be with God is life but to separate yourself from his presence is sure death. Our bodies that were perfect began to age and die. My spirit may be new in Christ but it's trapped in a world of decay and a body that continually tries to do opposite of God's will. To prove this, ever notice the wear and tear on our bodies or how we age? Ever let your spiritual guard down and find yourself doing something you know is not right to do? You were saved when you accepted Christ into your heart and life, however that did not stop the destruction and decay of our bodies or the world around us. We still experience the pain and groaning of our human condition. But the end of this groaning will happen when Jesus appears and makes all things new. Paul puts it this way in Romans 8:19-23 and notice the emphasis I placed:

The creation waits in eager expectation for the sons of God to be revealed. For the creation was subjected *to frustration*, not by its own choice, but by the will of the one who subjected it, in hope that the creation itself will be *liberated from its bondage to decay* and brought into the glorious freedom of the children of God. We know that the whole creation has been groaning as in the pains of childbirth *right up to the present time*. Not only so, but we ourselves, who have the first fruits of the Spirit, groan inwardly as we wait eagerly for our adoption as sons, the *redemption of our bodies*.

With this death and decay come all the problems associated with it like disease and infections. No one is exempt. No one. No race, no sex, no country, no culture, and no age; children are not even exempt, and that's one of the hardest things to bear in this life. The content of what Paul is saying is this, Christ makes us alive if He is in us and all the universe is waiting for our new bodies and the mature children of God to rule and reign with Christ; however our mortal body and this current earth is under a curse and is still dying. The complete redemption of our bodies comes later and we are waiting for that day; in the meantime, we groan like a woman in childbirth. If we have hope in Christ, one day we will be raised with a new body as Christ himself was raised, with a new body and eternal life.

This will happen when God makes all things new again and there will be no more curse (Rev. 21:5). Glory to God! I'm looking forward to that day! Yet, I must say, if you have not yet acknowledged that you have sinned and have not asked Christ into you heart and life, then you are dead spiritually *and* physically and that means you won't wake to eternal life but into judgement. I want to encourage you right now to put your hope in Christ and ask Him to come into your heart and give you a hope and a life no one can take away. If you need help with praying that prayer go back to the end of Chapter 1, and pray that prayer of salvation with me. If you *know* you are a son or daughter of God read on!

God Gave Man Dominion and Free Choice

God gave man free choice and with that great responsibility comes the consequences. With dominion over all the earth and freedom to choose, man has the potential to choose the greatest good and with that comes the ability to choose evil. When we choose poorly, we suffer the consequences of choosing our own way outside of God's will and divine plan for our lives. Sometimes the effects of our choices are damaging not only to ourselves but others around us and sometimes our choices can last for generations at a time. Adam and Eve's choice handed us a curse we didn't ask for and we begin our own lives by being born into it. If God is going to give us the power and authority, then God also lets us reap the consequences of our actions and doesn't run around cleaning up our messes on an individual basis.

God doesn't cause any child to die of disease; that is an effect of our choices handed down to us through mankind. God didn't cause my sister-in-law to get cancer; God didn't cause our loved ones to die in the war, they were there on the battlefield or in a conflict in harms way and fell to the circumstances of war. God didn't cause our spouse to leave us for another nor did God cause our friend to die in an accident. Okay, "I know that" you say, *I know God didn't put that sickness on that child, but He could have saved him.* If God went around forcing Himself and His will on others He wouldn't be a loving Father, He would be a dictator. Also God always uses the bad situations to bring about the greatest good (Romans 8:28). Just because we don't see or understand everything doesn't mean God is not working on our behalf. **Our job is not to control, but to trust Him through it all**. However, I find we get angry not necessarily at the problem we face, but because we know God has the power to stop it, and we feel He should. *We* are not the judge and any judgment we make is limited to our own point of view, for we are "the made" not the Maker, we are "the clay" not the Potter. We are "the orchestra" not the Conductor, we are "the creation" not the Creator.

The Glass Bubble is Broken

If I am going to get in an automobile and get out on the high way, I run the risk of being in an accident like anyone else, possibly killed. And it's safe to say, I'm not riding in a car with a force field around me like I'm in some protected Holy Ghost bubble. If I stick my hand in a fire I will get burned, if I'm outside in the cold wet rain, I run the chance of getting sick. If I surf or I'm swimming in a pool, I could drown. Even if I own a pool it's possible my neighbor's child could wander from their home when they're not looking and fall in and drown. *Such was the case in my own city last year and it happened to a Pastor's grandchild.* If I fly in a plane, it could crash. Both Christians and non-Christians were in the World Trade Center on September 11, 2001. Both Christians and non-Christians were on the planes the terrorist used as weapons to strike fear into us.

However cause and effect, sowing and reaping aside, things just happen and that's just it. Life is unpredictable and aren't we glad? What makes us think we are protected or special? Why do we think we will all live to be 100 years old and die in our sleep upon our beds? Where do we get that from? God never said that. Why do we think life is supposed to be fair or even perfect? God did not promise if you follow him everything will be easy and things will go your way nor did he say," I'll protect you from all harm." Actually it's quite the opposite, you will be tested and face great persecution and it's a test to the finish (James 1:12). God is a refiner and there is a fire. God is also an assayer and He tests the motives and purity of our metal (our heart). God uses those tough situations (the fire) to test us and refine our faith as silver and gold. However, not even God has promised us the next 3 seconds of our life. Everyday is a gift. It is written in *Hebrews 9:27*, *"Just as man is destined to die once, and after that to face judgment,"* and listen also to *Ecclesiates 3:2, "There is a time to be born and a time to die."* In both scriptures it guarantees we will die but it never tells us when. No one is promised tomorrow, but what you believe while you live and what you believe when you die makes all the difference in the world.

Why Does God allow bad things to happen to good people?

We have already looked at why bad things happen; it comes as the result of consequences from poor choices of our free will. Man has free will, and when we do things opposite of God, it will hurt us every time, not by or through God, but through our own choice. But why does God allow bad things to happen to good people? Not that I'm an expert but I want to share with you what I have learned since my "screaming at God" in my prayer closet trials. God allows the floods in our lives so that you will draw closer to Him. Odds are you wouldn't think twice about God if not for the flood that is bearing down on you. We run or look for a stable high ground when the floods come, thus drawing close to God. That is what it's all about, intimacy with God. It's why He sent His Son to die for us in the first place; to bring us back to His side. **Nothing else matters**. I've seen people in emergency rooms that don't have the first clue about God, fall to their knees, (usually *for the first time in their life*,) to ask God to save their son's life. There is something on the inside of us all that, when trials come, our instinct is to run to the maker and lover of our soul. In a time of need, our very soul or being cries out to the one that made us. Sometimes God uses difficult circumstances to get our attention focused where it should be all the time. Think about the times when you didn't have a clue who God was and when something happened, did you pray to Him? I know I did, I look back at it now and realize even then He was with me and was merciful to me.

God uses the fire to change us into the image of His son.

Make no mistake about it. You will be tried and there is no escaping it. As you have read a few paragraphs back, God is the great refiner of man. Those who are called according to His purpose will be put to the test. No exceptions. We want to be like Jesus and the only way to do that is through suffering and obedience through the trials. Jesus learned his own obedience through suffering

(Hebrews 5:8). We are being made into the pattern that is
Jesus Christ and if we are going to share with Him in His
glory, we will share with Him in His sufferings (Phil 3:10
and 2 Cor 1:7). Paul wrote this in Philippians 1:29, "For
to you, it has been granted on behalf of Christ, not only to
believe in Him, but also to suffer for His sake."

The apostle Peter tells us in 1Peter 1:7, that we are
molded and shaped by the fire, and our faith gets tested
like gold is tested. The heat of our circumstances gets
turned up and all the trash that was in us, or *dross*, floats
to the surface and is discarded. That is how gold becomes
pure. Then the fire is heated up again and this process is
repeated until all the impurities are out and nothing is
left but pure gold. Before long the image of the one doing
the refining can be seen in our lives. A great example of
this can be seen in the book of Daniel Chapter 3 with the
story of Shadrach, Meshach, and Abed-Nego. They were
under trial and stayed close to God. Their lives were
even threatened and they chose not to succumb to the
circumstances around them. They kept their eyes on God.
They get bound (helpless in their situation) and thrown
into the fire (the trial they're facing). Their faith in God
does not waiver and, when the King (God) looks in the fire,
he sees a form of another man and it looks like the image
of the son of God! Then they get pulled from the fire and
promoted! Would they have received their salvation in
the end if they had bowed to their circumstances? Would
they have survived the fire if they cursed God for their

predicament? Absolutely not! Instead they set their face like flint and said to themselves and to God, "**I don't understand what's going on here but I'm not going to walk away from my God because He has the power to save me and, even if He doesn't save me, I'm going to trust Him anyway**." The problem is most people walk away and only serve or love God when He is doing what they want Him to do for them. In their ignorance of God's ways, they trade their long-term salvation for something temporary.

I ask you again, will you trust God or will you walk away?

Naked I came from my mother's womb, and naked shall I return there. The Lord gave, and the Lord has taken away; Blessed be the name of the Lord." ~ Job (Job 1:21)

Christians today are under the misconception that once they walk up an aisle and say a prayer of salvation, they are now on auto-pilot and all they have to do is sit back on their blessed assurance and occasionally look up for Jesus who is coming back to take them away to a far away happy place of bliss. The truth is actually quite different.

For James 1:12 says very plainly, "Blessed is the man who *endures temptation*; for *when* he has been *proved*, he will receive the crown of life which the Lord has promised to those who *love* Him." (NKJ) Author's Emphasis.

The Word says when a man has been *proved he receives the reward.* We are tested and must be proved, we are tempted and tried and those who endure will receive the crown at the end. Who gets this crown? Those who love Jesus. Jesus constitutes our love for Him as one who obeys His commandments, (John 14:15, John 14:23). However, it is possible to lose our reward, so trust God and stay close to Him.

Why am I telling you this? Because if you feel you have been hurt by God, then you have faced a hardship and a trial and it is important for your faith to stay focused on God. Our anger towards God is misdirected through a lack of understanding. God is not responsible for your hardship but God will use your pain in bringing about a greater destination and reward for you. Don't short circuit what God is doing in you by walking away or giving up. Our job is to trust Him through it all and stay focused on Him no matter what fire is testing us or has tested us. After it is all over it will all make sense and we will see from the other end what God was doing on His end, but right now all we see is just a part of the story. It is all going to plan by the one that made the plan, and each strand of fabric of our life is being woven into a great beautiful tapestry of glory for the Father. In the end we will see the reward was greater than any suffering or hardship we ever endured here in this life.

I want to end this chapter with encouragement designed just for you. God loves you and He wants the best for your life. I can't begin to personally understand the pain that you felt during your trial that wounded you, but I want to encourage you to put your trust in God. He knows you better than you know yourself and has the best for you so take Him at His word and let go of the pain or anger you feel towards Him. Also, I want you to know that the same sorts of trials are being experienced by everyone else throughout the world. The fire comes on us all. How will you respond to it? Will you turn and walk away or will you be like Shadrach, Meshach and Abed-Nego and stare the fire in the face and say, "Lord, I don't understand you, I don't know why you let this happen, I don't know why I'm going through this, but I am going to trust You and love you anyway and I throw myself at your mercy." Amen!

Prayer

Lord, forgive me for blaming you. I understand you didn't cause this thing to happen but You are using it to draw my attention back to you. Please forgive me for all things I said against You from my heart and lips in the past, in the present and for the future I ask for your grace and understanding as I grow in my understanding of You. I want our relationship with each other renewed and I ask You to repair the hurt I felt as I give You my wounds. In Jesus' name, Amen.

CHAPTER
9

ABBA FATHER

A book on the subject of forgiveness is not complete without a chapter on fathers. This could be the most important chapter of this book for some of you. I know this because just yesterday I heard the Holy Spirit speak to my heart and say, "I want you to write a chapter just on fathers." That's what He spoke to my heart and I knew what He meant, and what He wanted. It shows the importance of our relationship with our fathers if the God of the universe wants a chapter devoted to one subject alone. Out of all the wounds caused by a loved one, the ones that hurt the most are the wounds caused by our fathers.

The Wound

James grew up in the big city where his father, John, moved his wife while 6 months pregnant, along with James and the family dog. Work was scarce back home so John packed up the family including the dog and headed to the big city. John got lucky and landed a first shift job at the tire factory slinging tires seven days a week, from seven to seven. Every two weeks, he got 3 days off. The pay would be great where they came from but in the big city the long 12 hour work days were needed to even out the higher cost of living. Worst yet, John began to miss out on his son's and daughter's life, but in his mind he was providing for his family and that's what mattered. "*You've got to be the best and have the best*," was the saying heard around the house when he was home. "*If you don't have the best you are nothing.*" John was feeling the pressure of caring for a second child and soon he was working a second job so he could lead the family in the direction he felt they should go.

In his mind, he was demonstrating sacrifice and leadership and instilling into his son a strong work ethic so he will have the skills in life to provide and lead his family. John never noticed he was missing his son's life altogether: No little league baseball games, no help with his son's school work, no advice on dating. He wasn't there at the dinner table or to help run the bath water. He was absent from his son's life altogether. James's life was without the affection of his father and James's life was void of a father's love and presence. John's long hours at work separated him from his wife and soon their intimacy grew cold. Bitterness, jealously, lack of trust along with a lack of communication with his wife led John to finding medication for his troubles in a bottle.

Soon he found himself drunk, in stronger, louder arguments, committing verbal and physical abuse to his family, in a hotel bedroom with a woman not his wife. Soon he found himself divorced. His family could not take the strain any longer. James, now age seven, could not figure out what he had done. He always thought it was his fault. It must be his fault. His father always spent his time at work or when he did come home, in front of the television or working on his car. Promise after promise was broken. Dad promised his son a tree house, Dad promised to throw the football, Dad promised to take his son fishing. John always felt he was showing love and compassion because he was providing for his family.

All James wanted was a hug, love and affection from his father and just to know his father cared and that he was doing okay in his father's eyes. When James went to bed at night, he would lie in bed thinking about life when the front door would open and before he could hear a voice, he could smell the alcohol making its way underneath the door. Soon he could hear his mother and father arguing through their bedroom wall. John would blame everyone but himself for his condition and soon He was cussing out his children, his spouse and even God above. "What did I do for God to curse me with such a lousy life?" "It's those *#&%* children of yours." "I'm not sure they're even mine. They couldn't be mine. James is lazy and absolutely worthless."

The day John and Mary got divorced, John tore into the house like a tornado to gather some remaining things. James went into his father's bedroom to see his father pack his things. "Dad, are you coming back? Where are you going?" With his next sentence John will cut his son so deeply it will echo through his son's life. "If you're a good boy I'll come back."

Only Our Father Can Validate Us

Don't make the mistake and think this real-life everyday American story is about boys and their fathers. It's about children and their fathers. Girls are not exempt, they are equal. Ever heard of daddy's little girl? This is why our fathers are so important to us as children. Your father and *only* your father can validate you. I will say this again and listen very carefully in case you are one of those skimmer readers. Only your father can validate you. The love of our mothers is special and we have a special maternal bond grounded in love, but it's our fathers that validate our life. It's our fathers that tell us, "It's okay. I love you, you're doing great! I'm here for you, I am constant and my love doesn't change." "You're okay and I love you." Our mothers can love and caress us and try to fill that need deep down in our soul. She can tell her son, "you're my big man", and help her daughter with boys and give advice and tell how beautiful she is, but nothing satisfies our soul until we hear our father express through word or deed "you're okay and I love you."

We need acceptance and love from our father. We need to know we are okay and our father is the only one who can do that. This very cry from the core of our being comes from being created from our heavenly Father above.

He is the creator of life and all life is from Him and created to worship Him. We get our very core of being from the creator of life. He created the flower but the flower needs the sun to survive. Then God made man in His image. He made man, not woman, first. He created woman out of man but man was created first and carries the power and seed to give life. The Word of God tells us that even man (Adam) gave names to all the livestock, birds and beast of the field as the Lord brought them to man to see what he would name them. What he called that animal is what it was from that day forward. Adam was made in the image of God and given power over all God had created. When the creatures came to him to be validated, he called them what they were. We go to our earthly father with the same longing to know who we are and with the power and authority God has placed unto our fathers; but we hear from them, "You're stupid." "You'll never make it." "You're as smart as an ox." "Why can't you do this?" "Why can't you be more like your brother?" It's no wonder our very soul cries out for longing of the acknowledgment of our heavenly father. We are still waiting and crying out for the acceptance we long for. We need to be truly validated.

Our heavenly Father is perfect, but our earthly father is human and makes mistakes. Growing up I was raised in a Christian household and I had a wonderful father and mother. However my father is not perfect and makes mistakes and will continue to make mistakes. No earthly father is perfect and no matter how hard they try not to, they will hurt their children; they will wound their children.

Maybe you are like James in the story we just read. Your father poured into you that if you aren't the best you're a failure, so you find yourself living today seeking the approval of your father, wife, boss, and world. Nothing you do is good enough, and you are emotionally and physically tired. Maybe your father promised you something and backed out, and you have held it against him all your life. He promised he would go see you play in the football game but that night, during your big play of the game, there was an empty seat in the stands where your father should have been. Maybe you grew up entirely without the love of a father and have never known the love embrace of a father figure in your life. We all need that love. Maybe he never would let you have that pet you begged him for and he repeatedly told you no. Was your father a harsh man? Did he live hard and play hard? Did he leave a tornado-sized wake behind him in everything he did?

Our fathers sometimes have the knack of knowing what "not to say" at the exact moment they should not say it. They cut us to the very core, and we carry the hurt around today buried deep in our heart and let it affect our life. Most of the time we think we are over it. Have you been hurt by your father and you swore either aloud or silently to yourself you would never do that to your children? Chances are you have never dealt with that wound and you are still carrying that hurt around trying to avoid it by living the opposite way. You can't avoid or change what happened by projecting your own hurt into the upbringing of your own children. This problem is a vicious cycle that must be dealt with for healing to occur in your life and theirs.

Hurting People Hurt People
Healed People Help Hurting People

Once again your wound affects your way of living and how you view life. Meanwhile you are creating hurt in your own children's lives in different ways. Believe me, that hurt didn't get healed; it's just been suppressed and ignored all these years. You just suppressed and ignored it and it resurfaced in another way and area of your life. My friend, we must face and acknowledge those hurts so we can be healed from them and have a healthy life. *We* must be healed first so we can help others that are hurting. Suppressing and finding those hurts resurfacing is like trying to push an inflated bright-colored beach ball underneath the water. Oh you may push the brightly-colored beach ball down temporarily. You think by sitting on it you have done a good job mastering it and hiding it for years, but it's coming back up and it just might pop up unexpectedly in a place you're not ready for.

Like that beach ball underneath the water, the hurt is there; it's coming up and it just might pop up anywhere.

I want to encourage you my friend, you need to face that wound or hurt in your past. You can do this with God's help and He is standing by to begin your healing process. Face those things your father did to you and give it to the One who can heal you and make you whole again. But first we are going to look at how the hurts in our life caused by our earthly father have twisted the view of our Heavenly Father.

The Great Deception

One of Satan's primary weapons against mankind is deception. He has honed the craft of spinning the truth and warping it over many years. Always remember it is warped from the inside out. He takes a truth and spins it warping it from the center. He wants you to have a twisted view of your Heavenly Father and sever your relationship from your life source and personal creator. Whether we have realized this or not our view of our earthly father can warp our view of our Heavenly Father. Do you feel you have a healthy view of your Heavenly Father? If you had a harsh and tough father at home, he lived hard and played hard, and someone wanted you to introduce you to the Heavenly Father, what do you think your view on fathers is going to be? How could it be any different from what you have come to know as what a father is? If I say the word "father," what pops into your mind? In fact, close your eyes for a moment and let your heart be still.

Now when you have done that say the word "Father God." What thoughts and feeling come to mind? Is God a harsh man to you? Do you feel you are on His good side when you perform for Him, and He is angry with you when you don't? Do you feel you are trying to live up to God and make Him happy so He can be pleased with you? Does God seem distant and void in your life? Do you think He is displeased with you, ready to bash you in the head verbally or physically if you did something wrong? Are you seeking God's approval? Or when you closed your eyes and said "Father God," does peace and love come to you? Comfort and warmth and a sweet presence of assurance? Did you think of mercy and grace? Whether you thought harsh things or good things, I have some wonderful news for you! I want to tell you the truth about your True Father.

Do you remember that time you made that touchdown or made a great tackle on the football field and you thought no one saw it? Someone did, your Father. Do you remember that great play you did on the baseball field? The time you played the piano recital and you thought only one parent saw you? Someone did, it was your Heavenly Father, and do you know what? He was proud of you! I remember just where I was when I realized these things myself and finally came to the realization that I have never been alone, not once--- ever.

Do you remember the time your heart was broken by that boy or girl? God was there and His heart ached for you. He knows what it's like to be betrayed by someone you love and have your heart broken. The time your mother or father was diagnosed with terminal cancer, God was there and was with you through your entire struggle. He never once left your side. He never promised you it wouldn't rain, but He did promise to be there with you through it all.

I want to tell you the truth about your Heavenly Father. He is always merciful, good and fair and always keeps His word. That is one of my personal favorite attributes of our Father; He is faithful. He has proven that to me over and over. If He says something He means it and will stand by it now and forever. He is not like our earthly father that promised to take us fishing and never did. He is not like our earthly father that told us he loved us, kissed us good night and tucked us into bed only to run off with another woman in the morning because he felt he didn't want to be married or be a father anymore. Your heavenly Father thinks nothing but good thoughts toward you and loves to show mercy to all those who sincerely ask for it. He is near to the broken hearted and those who are hurting. He is not a hard task master or harsh king. His personality is gentle and kind. His commands are not troublesome or burdensome. You are the apple of His eye. You are His special treasure and He is your great reward. Even in your worst state and lowest point in your life, He loved you then as much as now. You can't earn His love. There is nothing you can do to make Him love you more than He does right now. Take a moment and think on that. *Say to yourself out loud "I can't earn God's love. My Father loves me!"*

I want to share with you a special moment between God and I. I awoke one night, eyes wide open and He was drawing me to Him. I had a strong pull in my heart to read Proverbs Chapter 3. I got up and turned on my light (If this ever happens to you don't fight it; just get up and say "here I am!"). I knelt down on my knees and I opened my Bible. God's presence was so strong in my room; He spoke to me directly through His Word. Proverbs 3 started off with, "My son." I said, "Father, I love it when you call me son", and He spoke back very plainly to me, "I love it when you call me Father!" That surprised me! Then he said, "Do you see those pictures over there?" I turned to see what He was referring to. He was referring to some of my old school portrait pictures I had found earlier that week of a long time ago in my life. At that time, I was so lost and didn't know Him.

I really don't know why, but I had stuck them across my mirror in chronological order. He said, "I loved you then, as I love you now." I was blown away by God's love and grace. He did love me then. At a time I thought no one cared or even knew I was breathing, He was there. All this time my studying, good works and theology degrees didn't bring me closer to Him. It didn't matter how much sin I eliminated from my life. He loved me through it all. He loves you regardless. He loves me through the process of growing in Him. God does not have favorites! Your Heavenly Father wants you and is pursuing you.

There are times when He wakes me up just to hang out with me because He loves the company. He wants the same with you! He wants to be in your presence as well. We always think of it as being in *His* presence because it is hard for us to think that *He*, God of the Universe, wants to be with *us*. Why? Because He loves you!

Your Father is not just a good father, He is a perfect one. He owns the cattle on a thousand hills and the hills too, but more important to Him in the entire world is **you**. He is not like James' father, John, from the beginning of the chapter. God loves you regardless whether you think you failed today or not. Even if you didn't get something done for the corporate church or reach your goal to lead 20,000 people to the Lord (or even 1) this year, your Father in heaven loves you still. He does not love you more for all the things you do for Him. We serve, fear and obey Him because we love Him. We love Him first and then can't help to do everything else. He loves you for who you are just like we love Him for who He is, not for what He can give us. He doesn't love you and want to be with you to get something out of you. We are accepted by His grace. Trust God our Father with your heart. He won't let you down.

It's Time to Let Go and Trust God

I want you to take a big step with me and let go of the hurt your earthly father has caused you. It's time. Forgiveness is sometimes a process so it might not happen all at once--- or it might! But one thing is for certain. Jesus said, "When you pray, believe you will receive them and you will have them"(Mark 11:24). Let's start the healing right now. Let God have that wound so He can heal you. Some of you are still running. Some are still denying. Let it go. Your Heavenly Father is standing by and with you now, wanting to heal you. As always I will encourage you to pray this prayer with me. You can read over it first so you can understand what God wants or what we need to acknowledge so we can be healed.

We must acknowledge the particular hurt they have caused us and how they made us feel. Be honest and say it and then give it to God. Maybe you felt abandoned, say "God, my father was never there and I have always felt unloved or abandoned." Or, "My father told me he hated me and that broke my heart." "My father told me he would take me to the ball game and he never did." "I hated the way he talked to mom and how he left us." "It hurt that He considered work more important than me." Please, be honest with God so He can heal you. Those areas will have a blank in them for you to fill. If you need more space just get out some more paper. Let's pray.

Heavenly Father. Thank you for being by my side and being here, thank you for never leaving me nor forsaking me and being true to your Word. I am here to let you have all the pain my father caused me. You told me to forgive so I could be forgiven, so I come before you to release the pain my father caused me. My father hurt me by_____
_____ and that made me feel_____
_____.

I forgive my father for what he did, and I release it to you. I give you the wound and ask for total healing in my life. I now release my father from what he did to me and how he made me feel. I ask you to please forgive me and show me all the ways this has affected my life so I can begin to change them and become better in my walk with you as your child, a husband and father or friend. I want you to be my true father and show me your love as my Daddy God. I thank you for touching this wound and I give it to you with my whole heart. In Jesus' name I pray, Amen.

CHAPTER
10

FORGIVING LEADERS OF THE CHURCH

he deepest wounds come from those closest to us; thereby hurting us the most. The deepest and most damaging wounds in our heart that affect our lives are usually from a parent or family member. However, right on the heels of hurt from those that raised us are those we trust where we gather to worship. Whether you serve on staff in a ministry full time, part time or you just volunteer your time when you can, if you have been truly hurt by those in leadership position in the church, this chapter is for you.

Understanding Delegated Leaders
Who They Are. Who They Aren't.

When I say hurt from leaders, I'm not talking about you're upset with the Pastor because he didn't know your name after two months of attending the church. I'm not referring to the time the worship leader wouldn't let you sing the song the Lord laid on your heart or the time the Pastor just didn't see or recognize "the anointing" or "gifts" in your life.

I'm talking about being truly wronged and suffering at the hands of ignorance by some of the leaders God has placed over us. Yes, God Himself is the one that places those men or women over us in their leadership role and you have heard it takes all kinds to make the world go round. Yes, there are wicked leaders out there. God didn't put them in authority because they were wicked, but they themselves abuse their leadership usually for their own glory and they will be dealt with harshly if they do not relent. Judgment always begins with the house of God and every man, whether in the ministry or not, will have to one day give account to God about what they did with what God gave them. Not one thing done or one thing said is hidden in the sight of God. He is the one and only Judge.

I find also there are leaders who hurt people unintentionally through ignorance of God's ways and laws. Always remember, just because they are called to minister doesn't make them Superman or knowledgeable in every area and subject. Being called to ministry means they are called to serve you in the manner of Christ. Serving is the very definition of ministry. They *minister* to you and serve *you*. It does not mean they know it all or they are perfect or have a closer walk with God than anyone else. **Ministers do not have a closer walk with God because of their called position**. But if you are not mindful, some ministers will let you continue to think they do. Sometimes they even fool themselves in that manner.

Always remember **ministry does not equal**

relationship. Ministers are God's delegated authority called by God Himself to serve the body of Christ (you) through the direction of Jesus Christ. Pastors are human beings and are not perfect and make mistakes all the time. I served as an Associate Pastor in my local church and I have experience in mistakes, being gun-ho, jumping the gun, and being human. I wonder often, why do we have a higher expectation of ministers than ourselves? We expect them to be perfect when they are not and don't have the capacity to do so, so then the problem comes when we look at the person and not the office in which they hold. That is how God sees them, through the office in which they hold. I don't put my trust in any man; I put my trust in the Lord. **Psalm 118:8** says, "It is better to take refuge in the Lord than to trust in man."

That is why Pastors never disappoint me when things go wrong in their personal life, church life or my life. Before I joined the church I now attend, I was having lunch with the Senior Pastor and he said, "Jason, sooner or later I'm going to disappoint you or let you down." My reply was, "You won't let me down because I don't put my trust in you, I put my trust in the Lord!" That wasn't a put down on my Pastor; he is a good man. I was letting him know where the boundaries are and where my hope and trust lie. Don't misunderstand me; we don't cover our hurt with excusing leaders from their actions with an excuse of "they're only human." We have learned earlier not to excuse our hurts or wounds; what we *are* doing is getting

understanding of their position before we look at the
scriptures on how to handle mistreatment.

Understanding the boundaries of those placed in
authority over us will help us walk out our forgiveness
for them. We must get understanding. We must honor
the man or woman God has placed in charge over us;
but we are honoring the position, not the man. The *man* is
human and, like you, is redeemed but capable of making
mistakes. Some wounds and hurts that come from those
placed in authority are deeper because we have the wrong
idea of them to begin with. *They* are not God; they *serve* God
and serve you. We err when we put man on a pedestal or
place them on the throne instead of God. God's delegated
authorities are supposed to *always* get their direction from
God; but from time to time, "being only human", they
get ahead of themselves or become confident in the Lord
or their relationship, and feel they can make decisions on
their own though they haven't sought His opinion. Or they
speak for God when God has been silent (See Proverbs 3).
What results is the ministers speaking from their flesh, in
their own feelings, or a lack of understanding and thus
wounding those around them. It's not unusual for those
who are new to ministry to leave a large wake of dead and
wounded behind them.

It Wasn't God That Hurt You

My dear friend if you don't get anything else from

this chapter, if you just get this one thing it will be worth while. **God did not hurt you.** It was the man or woman behind the office. What makes my heart break when thinking about wounds from church leaders is this: the wounded are left with the twisted impression that God is the one that did this to them. Maybe you think it was God's judgment, or you were bad in His eyes and you had it coming to you, or that is God's way or nature. That was not God; that was man! That is what hurts the most about the Catholic sexual abuse scandals. Thousands of children were mistreated and sexually abused across many decades by those they trusted with their spiritual lives and those that were supposed to be representing God. Those very children grew up lost inside not feeling they could turn to God for their strength or help. If they couldn't turn to God, then where could they turn? I could not think of a more damaging true life scenario. I could not think of anything that breaks the heart of God more or kindles the flames in His eyes more. Listen to what Jesus Himself says about children in Matthew 18:5:

And whoever welcomes a little child like this in my name welcomes me. But if anyone causes one of these little ones who believe in me to sin, it would be better for him to have a large millstone hung around his neck and to be drowned in the depths of the sea.

Worse still was the punishment issued when the

abuse was discovered. Nothing was done. Not until it hurt the Catholic Church financially did they react. Maybe you can't relate if you're not Catholic. I myself am not; however, you don't have to be from a Catholic background to be hurt by those in authority or to understand betrayal.

Mega Canned Theology

All across the United States there is a great movement in the modern church era; the American churches are adopting an idea of a vision placed on the walls in the church building for all to see. The initial reasoning of posting this vision comes from the scripture from Habakkuk 2:1 which reads, *"Write the vision and make it plain on tablets, that he may run who reads it"*(NKJV). That is great. We need vision for us to know where we are going and we need to receive the vision from God. Is that practice wrong? No. However, I have seen visions turn into religious juggernauts that crush, grind and spit out the very saints of God the vision is supposed to be for. This juggernaut machine is fed by vanity, the flesh and a daily dose of the mega church down the road or on your own television set 24 hours a day. **Unless the Lord builds the house you labor in vain! (Psalm 127:1)** They see a blue print for a pathway to prosperity and run with it. Not once asking God what He has planned specifically for them. We are all one body, but is the foot now trying to be the hand? Each church is turning into the other, copying an already-made blue print of how a church is supposed to *look* and behave, the bigger the better. The stamped plan is broadcast like a light on a buoy blinking continually for you to covet till you have arrived. On the local scale if you don't line up with the vision personally then you're an outcast. You just don't fit in to where they want to go. There's no longer any need for you if you can't adjust to where they are trying to get to. I have some breaking news for everyone; we can't fit God into a one-size-fits-all box! You can't have canned religion (God in a box with big screens and a *Hillsongs* praise team!). When will we learn we can't pull God's strings?

If you are a minister or leader in a church, this message is for you. **The vision is always for the people, not people for the vision!** In other words, you need a vision for the people, not people for the vision. Each one should come from God --- the vision and the people. God gives us the vision; He will give you the people and the way to carry it out in His time. It's God's responsibility, and He will fulfill it and show us how to walk out the vision. However, children of the King are being trampled daily by the "vision of excellence" movement, placed like a yoke on the shoulders of His children, and this is not going unnoticed by God. The true form of excellence is generated first from the inside of us and then begins to show on the outside. If you take away the presence of God then all you have is a form of godliness. His presence cannot be renewed, generated or conjured through outward godliness but must start, progress, and end with God alone. In the same sense, a spirit of excellence cannot be formed from the outside but formed on the inside.

A *spirit* or *form* of excellence is created by God *only* from the inside of His servants' hearts; not placed on the shoulders as a yoke by other servants. We can't order someone to be excellent. We might as well snap our fingers and command each other to be Holy. Holiness, excellence and God's presence is brought about not through written vision on walls, but through an intimate personal relationship that can only be wrought by the flames on the hot anvil *over time* by the Holy consuming fire himself, Jesus Christ. It should be Jesus-driven, not ministry-driven. Corporate church should also be relationship-driven, not ministry-driven. Always keep in mind; God is interested in His people, not our ministry. God is not about our ministry or what we have done or what you can do for Him (which is zip, zero, zilch, anyway). He is about relationships and intimacy with his beloved, His bride. Always remember, if God can use a donkey to preach a message then it's not about us!

I want to mention one thing more before I get off my soap box and look at the scriptures on how to handle mistreatment from church leaders. You may have picked up by now that these churches that follow each other and drive their people to catch up to the other are a sore spot with me. Am I against mega churches? Absolutely not. There are several in my home town and I love them all.

I personally think God is making some church buildings bigger today so when the end time turmoil really hits the fan, *which has already started,* people will fear and flock by the thousands into the local church to seek help. We need to have somewhere for them to go and thousands trained to minister to them. However, I have a problem with each church looking at the other and being influenced by one another (see 2 Corinthians 10:12). We are supposed to always look up, not around us.

I look at it like this. John Bevere, author of *the Bait of Satan* and *Drawing Near,* is one of my favorite speakers. I remember the first time I saw him in person I thought, *"Wow, what a man of God, that's how I want to be. That's where I want to go someday. I hope to be like him someday."* The Holy Spirit jumped in and said, "I don't need another John Bevere. I already have one; I need a Jason Canady!" I erred by looking at man as my example. **Jesus** is the pattern we are supposed to be molded into. I took my eyes off of Jesus for a moment and looked at the man, and then compared myself to him and instantly coveted his status. Would I have continued to the next phase, I would likely have gone about doing things the way John Bevere did.

You see, God already has a Billy Graham, T.D. Jakes, Joel Olsteen, and Joyce Myers or that great pastor in that big church down the road. He needs you. You are unique and have a destiny all of your own. We are supposed to get our daily bread and direction from God. We err when we look around and compare ourselves with our brothers and sisters and look to what God is doing in their life or with their church. The same principle applies with copying each other as churches when God has personally called forth and placed each church in that particular area for a particular reason.

How Do I Handle The Unfair Treatment From My Leader?

When someone comes to me with complaints about their Pastor, I tell them something they are shocked to hear and even more reluctant to do. I ask, "Do you really want to see a change in your Pastor?" "Yes. I sure do," is always the reply. "Then pray for him!" The hardest thing to do for someone that has hurt you is to pray for them or, in other words, bless them. That is exactly what we are doing. It is opposite of the way we feel but that's our flesh and our flesh is against God. Praying for our leaders is a principle of God. We love our enemies and pray for them. Anything that the enemy uses or tries against us, goes right back to them. We bless those that curse us and God moves in miraculous ways.

Prayer for those placed over us is scriptural and also our duty. Let's look at it in 1Timothy 2:1

> I urge, then, first of all, that request, prayers,
> intercession and thanksgiving be made for
> everyone- for kings and all those in authority,
> that we may live peaceful and quiet lives in all

godliness and holiness.

Have you been hurt by those placed in authority? Here are some biblical principles and sure-fire ways I have used that have made a big difference in my personal relationship with God and my personal walk as a Christian. Just keep in mind these two steps.

Step One. Pray for that person that wronged you. I know it sounds hard. When we pray during our morning time with God, we are supposed to lift up those in authority over us to God and intercede on the behalf of our brother or sister. Let me ask you this question and answer it to yourself. Do you want to change the hurtful situation for the good or do you want revenge for what they did to you? There is something special that takes place when you pray for those that hurt you, especially those in authority over you. Praying for them releases something very powerful to work on your behalf. It's the Spirit of God! You change first! I have found praying for those that wronged us heals our wounds first, and then changes those we pray for. We have already read we are supposed to pray for our leaders. Let's read what Jesus says about our persecutors in Matthew 5:43-45.

> You have heard that it was said, 'Love your neighbor and hate your enemy.' But I tell you: Love your enemies and pray for those that persecute you, that you may be sons of your Father in heaven.

Step Two. Don't retaliate! Don't try and fight any battles in the flesh that can only be won in the Spirit! Whatever you do, don't defend yourself by word or deed. Let God defend you. Don't dare open your mouth in any defense thus tying God's hands from working on your behalf. He is a God of justice and the righteous judge. Give it to Him and let Him handle it. As children of God we should know God is in control and has the final authority to what happens to us. We understand as Christians and servants of God that our lives are fully in His hands, so we don't go picking and choosing times when we think our life should be in our hands. Let's go to the Word to see how Jesus, the pattern for our lives, handled mistreatment and false allegations by those in authority. In this passage of Matthew 26, they have just arrested Jesus and brought Him to Caiaphas, the high priest, who is the high authority of the temple. Let's start in verse 59:

> 59. The chief priests and the whole Sanhedrin were
> looking for false evidence against Jesus so they could put
> him to death. But they did not find any, though many
> false witnesses came forward. Finally two came forward
> and declared, "This fellow said, I am able to destroy the
> temple of God and rebuild it in three days."
> 62. Then the high priest stood and said to Jesus,
> "Are you not going to answer? What is this testimony
> that these men are bringing against you?"
> 63. **But Jesus remained silent**.

Next, let's look at how Jesus responded to Pilate in Matthew 27:12:

> 12. When **he was accused** by the chief priests and the elders, **he gave no answer**. Then Pilate asked him, "Don't you hear the testimony they are bringing against you?" But Jesus made no reply, not even to a single charge- to the great amazement of the governor. (Author's emphasis)

When He was accused - He gave no answer. Jesus didn't make a reply because He knew whose hands He was in. Also He was respecting God's delegated authority while being falsely accused. **Being falsely accused by those in delegated authority does not give us the right to go against God's delegated authority**. Being wounded or slandered by those in authority does not negate what God says about His authority. God will not hold us blameless if we speak against those He Himself has placed over us. Let's look one last time at the account with Pilate, this time as recorded in John 19: 9:

> "Where do you come from?" he asked Jesus, but Jesus gave him no answer. 10 "Do you refuse to speak to me?" Pilate said, "Don't you realize I have the power either to free you or to crucify you?"

11 Jesus answered, "You would have no power over me
if it were not given to you from above. Therefore the one
who handed me over to you is guilty of a greater sin."

The one that hurt you is the one that sinned. God
deals with each man and judges each man according to
their works and deeds. Let's respond appropriately in the
future so He may find us blameless. In Hebrews 5, it tells
us Jesus Himself learned obedience from what He suffered,
which in turn made Him perfect. You see, the suffering we
endure transforms us, hammers us, like a blacksmith to an
anvil and helps discipline us and mold us into the image
of God. God can take what happened to you and work it
together for good (Romans 8: 28).

The above solutions and scriptures are answers
based on wounds caused by slander and false accusations,
which is rampant in the church today. If you have been
severely wounded by a leader, those lessons still apply.
However, I want to let you know there is no way I nor can
anyone else truly know your pain or what you're going
through. But God does. I have seen and heard some of the
most awful things done in the environment of Church from
great monetary loss, to marital affairs and even murder. A
Pastor in a nearby city of mine strangled his wife last year
and rode her around in his trunk for days. On the surface
level, Christians kill their wounded because it looks bad
for their faith and (most *importantly of all)* their church. If
usher John is doing well, he is well liked, and everyone

loves usher John. Then they find out usher John is secretly fighting alcohol binges. Instead of Christians running to his aid they are running to the Pastor for his resignation. That doesn't look good for them, so out he goes. I have a reply to that. "Where's the love?"

Susan is single, eighteen and sings in the choir, one night she made a tragic mistake and gave into that boy's honey potion in her ear. She found out one time is all she needed to reap dire consequences and now she is pregnant. The last thing the choir wants is unwed teenager Susan standing up there praising God with a swollen belly. "Susan I'm sorry, but you have to step down. You understand." Translation: It looks bad for us; the choir is reserved for those that are holy. They don't see Susan on her face before God crying in repentance and pledging to do the right thing. They see a problem that looks bad in the eyes of those they are trying to attract and keep.

I could really tell you some sickening things about church life and you could no doubt tell me. The truth is I have had some deeper and much worse real life scenarios happen to people around me that when I heard of them, I broke down and cried for them. But I won't dare even use the worst illustrations for the fear of slander and speaking against who God has ordained. If you have been hurt by those in the church I want to tell you on behalf of Christians everywhere I am so sorry. God did not do that to you my friend and there is healing for you.

Maybe you suffered at the hands of a cruel man or woman

over you at church; a brother or sister or maybe a religious zealot slandered your reputation. Give the hurt to God and let Him heal the wound. I want you to reach out to God in faith and take Him at His Word. He is a good God and wants to heal your broken heart. Release it to Him and let Him work on your behalf. If you're willing and ready, let's go to His throne and find grace in time of need. Let's pray.

Heavenly Father,

Help me, I come to you in faith in the name of Jesus and I ask for your help in healing the pain that has been caused in my life by (offender's name/s). I understand you don't want me to defend myself but that You want that responsibility. So I fully release the situation to You right now and put it in Your hands. I ask you to bless (offender's name/s) with the knowledge and understanding that they might know you better. I ask you to bless them in Jesus' name. Now Father, I ask you to heal my heart and the wounds they caused me. Jesus, thank you for giving me your light, so that I may see. Thank you for loving me and working on my behalf. No matter what happens I know this situation is now in your care. In Jesus' name, Amen.

CHAPTER

11

THE UNFORGIVING SERVANT

Ephesians 4:32
And be kind to one another, tenderhearted, forgiving one another,
just as God in Christ also forgave you. ~ Paul

s the sun sets on our days of unforgiving, and as we begin to close our overall lesson of forgiveness, I would be a great injustice if I did not include the parable of the unforgiving servant recorded in Matthew 18. It is one of my favorite lessons and one that started my journey on the road to forgiveness. In Matthew 18:21, Peter asks Jesus, "How many times shall my brother sin against me, and I forgive him?" We know already Jesus' response of seventy times seven. However, Jesus launches into a very powerful example of how God the Father looks at the big picture of our own life, a life that includes sin, forgiveness, mercy, and redemption. I want to comment on this short parable from the New King James and share with you some of the revelation God has birthed in me. We will start with verse 23 as Jesus starts his lesson, "Therefore the kingdom of heaven is like a certain king who wanted to settle accounts with his servants." The *kingdom*, as Jesus puts

it, is you. It's not around you; it's in you. The kingdom
is also how God does things, it's what is expected of us
and is part of God's kingdom principles. God is the king
in this parable and we are the subjects in His kingdom.
Each of us has an account in His kingdom and there is
a day He will settle each account with each of us. Jesus
continues in verse 24:

24. "And when he had begun to settle accounts, one was
brought to him who owed him ten thousand talents.

25. "But as he was not able to pay, his master commanded
that he be sold, with his wife and children and all that he
had, and the payment be made.

The amount quoted that the servant owed was
an amount that at today's price would be in the billions.
Jesus picked an astronomical amount for the listeners to
understand the amount of debt that was against him. Now
here's a revelation God showed me. I used to think to
myself that this man deserved getting caught for running
up a debt so large. How ironic, *That is also the point of view most
Christians take of each other*. Maybe he was gambling, maybe
he thought he needed that large house and luxurious
Mercedes Benz. Maybe he started a business God didn't
tell him to start. Maybe he tried to live outside his means.
But the truth is, the servant could have had nothing to do
with the amount that was run up. He could have **inherited**
his debt and that is what God showed me, He inherited

this debt. It was the debt of sin that was on each one of us. It was a debt *we* could not pay back. "With his wife and children and all that he had," is a reference that shows this debt will cost you everything that belongs to you and means to you. It will cost you everything. The debt is the wages of sin and the payment to be made is death. Let's find out what the servant with the large debt he couldn't pay did about his situation. In verse 26, **"The servant therefore fell down before him, saying, 'Master, have patience with me, and I will pay you all.'"** So he did the only thing he could do and that was to throw himself at the mercy of who it was that has the power over life and death, particularly his own life. Verse 27 says**, "Then the master of that servant was moved with compassion, released him, and forgave him the debt.**

Wow! The master was moved with compassion! Doesn't sound like an angry master to me, but a merciful one. Also He didn't hold anything against the servant after He released him, His forgiveness was unconditional. This really shows the love of God for us, because He didn't set up a payment plan, He didn't say He forgave and held it against him. Most of us can't let even the little things go and this kind master (God) let a debt go completely that was in the billions! So what does this servant do? Verse 28 says, "But the servant went out and found one of his fellow servants who owed him a hundred denarii; and he laid hands on him and took him by the throat, saying. 'Pay me what you owe!'

Do you see what has happened? After the master had mercy on him and released him of the **greatest debt possible,** the servant runs out into his daily life and encounters another servant (our fellow brother or sister) who owes him such a small amount (anything next to the greatest debt is small) and demands that he get repaid the full amount. He does this angrily and without mercy. You can say that he has lost his perspective of the big picture. You can also say he doesn't grasp nor remember the mercy that was just shown to him. *So he loves little,* and is blind to God's grace to him.

Verse 29-30 say**,** "So his fellow servant fell down at his feet and begged him, saying, 'Have patience with me, and I will pay you all.' And he would not, but went and threw him into prison till he should pay the debt."

Once again, this is a classic case of a holier-than-thou attitude. This unforgiving servant takes the standpoint of wanting mercy for himself, but is quick to judge and condemn others. **This is the attitude and standpoint of most Christians**. I hate to write that but it's true. Just ask the lady that gives the evil eye to the teenager with a tattoo as he walks in on Sunday. Just ask the people who look down at other fellow servants who have experienced the pain of a divorce. Just ask those that point a finger to those of a different skin color or background than theirs. Just ask those that point their finger at others that struggle with addictions as they wonder "why can't they just get over it?" Just ask the ushers that show the young man to the door because he is wearing blue jeans or because he wears his hair longer than normal. Just take a look at this servant in this parable that is blind to God's grace and love for him, and has forgotten how his own salvation came about in the first place. He is not showing others the love and mercy that was shown to him.

Make no mistake about it, everything is seen and heard, from every idle word spoken to everything done in secret. Everything is seen by God and gets reported back to Him who judges rightly. We will see this in the next verse as we pick up after the unforgiving servant carried out his sentence to his fellow servant. Notice it says fellow servant and not brother or sister. Both the unforgiving servant and fellow servant could be any race, sex or creed.

Verse 31 says, "So when his fellow servants saw what had been done, they were very grieved, and came and told their master all that had been done."

It's time for another revelation God showed me. These other "fellow servants" in this parable are the angels and former saints of God. Remember what happened when John bowed down to the angel in Revelations, "And I fell to his feet to worship him. But he said to me, 'See that you do not do that! I am your fellow servant, and of your brethren who have the testimony of Jesus'" (Revelations 19:10).

Hear it from Jesus Himself in Matthew 18:10, "Take heed that you do not despise one of these little ones, for I say to you that in heaven their angels always see the face of My Father who is in heaven."

So the unforgiving servant was seen not showing mercy or love but forcing his will on another. Pay attention to how the unforgiving servant treated his brother or sister. Notice the judgment that was handed out. We will see this boomerang right back to the one that made the judgment. Let's find out what the master thought after this report got back to him about the servant who refused to forgive:

> 32. "Then his master, after he had called him, said to him, 'You wicked servant! I forgave you all that debt because you begged me. 33. 'Should you not also have had compassion on your fellow servant, just as I had pity on you?'

Listen to the passion expressed by the master. He is a compassionate master but when confronted with the truth of someone not forgiving or showing mercy after they themselves received mercy, He became angry. Here in this statement by the master is proof that God believes if mercy has been shown to us, God wants us to show mercy to others. Always keep in mind our own debt! Always remember you had a debt you could not pay yourself. I don't care how much money or things you gave away. I don't care if you worked in every soup kitchen in your town. I don't care if you helped widows, helped change every flat tire, or gave every homeless man a blanket. You could never pay off the debt of sin. The punishment for you was death! Yet you have been forgiven! You are debt free! Now, compare that debt against something someone did to you. Maybe they owe you 85,000 dollars. Compare that to the great debt. It pales in comparison. Maybe a family member was killed by a drunk driver and you can't let it go. Compare it to a debt you couldn't pay. Somebody said something to wound you deeply, or they stabbed you in the back. Compare the debts. Is there anything you can stack against the ultimate debt that could equal it? Now go show mercy the way God showed you mercy. **The Master** is about to hand the unforgiving servant the punishment for not forgiving others from his heart. Before we do, I want you to notice this is a **servant of God**, a Christian. Don't think this applies to those who aren't Christians. This parable is totally about Christians and how we are to love and treat each other. *To love* is Jesus' command to us. Let's see what happened in verse 34. "And his master was angry, and delivered him to the torturers until he should pay all that was due him."

Here is another example of Jesus' principle; the way you judge others is the way you are judged, and the measure of judgment you use against others is the same measure used to judge you. What did the unforgiving servant do to his fellow servant? He went and had him thrown in prison until the debt was paid! What then did the master do to that servant? Threw him into prison until he should pay all that was due him! So in the end the servant had a chance to show mercy but did not. He had a chance to forgive others and work out his own salvation. He did not. Here comes the warning by Jesus at the end of this parable to each of us. Pay close attention because Jesus is speaking this warning to you and I in verse 35, "So My heavenly Father also will do to each of you, if he, from his heart, does not forgive his brother his trespasses."

Jesus said, "from his heart." That is so important. We say we forgave that person for that hurt they caused us, but is that true? God can see into our very hearts and He knows the heart and mind of every man. He knows if we are just providing lip service or not when we say we forgive someone. My friend, please hear me when I say this. Most Christians have avoided the tough scriptures like this for many years and this warning from Jesus is not lip service; Jesus means what He says, and says what He means! **God the Father is absolutely adamant about us forgiving and loving one another**. We need to grow and come into the maturity Christ intends for us. We can't go on any further if we can't forgive. Our salvation is then a train with no track, a car with no motor, a gun with no bullets. It's a light bulb without electricity.

Most Christians are under the impression they can just sit back and be on auto pilot while waiting for Jesus. They pick which scriptures they choose to obey and can recite the blessing scriptures by memory while they overlook the commandments or warnings from God. **God forgives us and expects us to forgive others**. He is the Master in Jesus' parable and He is the Master of us now. We need to take forgiveness seriously. Time is running out. Let's not be caught napping or in complacency, but watchful when the master returns. Let us be found doing good and showing love and mercy to each other, not judging and condemning one another. Love will cover a multitude of sins!

My friend, there will not be a scenario whereby we sweep all the hurt and sin under a rug and we enter the kingdom of God anyway. For everything done and spoken under the sun will see the light of day. It will either be dealt with in this life or the next. It is important we deal with it now. Why? God gives us a chance to judge and deal with the sins ourselves. He rejoices when we come to Him for help and want to change or show mercy or do what is right. Second, if *we don't*, then he has to step in and do it for us. It is a fearful thing to fall into the hands of the living God (Hebrews 10:31)!

Third and last thing. Nothing impure, shameful or deceitful will enter the city of God (Revelation 21:27). Please don't be fooled. The Bride of Jesus, you and I, will be a bride without spot or wrinkle. She will be perfect and ready to walk down the aisle in all her glory to be with her beloved bridegroom. She won't have unfinished business hidden underneath her white dress! She won't have a hair out of place or her lipstick smudged. But she will be adorned with jewels of victory and will be perfect and pure in all her ways. A bride fit for a king, and not just any king, The KING OF KINGS!

For **everything** will be shaken and the only thing left are the things that can't be shaken. The heat will be turned up and every impurity burned away before the gold of our faith is pronounced pure! It will be said that the gold is so pure it is transparent (Revelation 21:18). I say again, everything will be dealt with now or later. So if you have made it this far without acknowledging your need of God and you can't say with a clean heart, "I have forgiven everyone," then I strongly urge you to lay it all down at the Master's feet. There is nothing more important or serious. God is ready to heal and help you. He can create in you a clean heart and a clear conscience. This is the final and last prayer we will go through together.

Heavenly Father,

I come before you and all of heaven through the name of Jesus. I come to find grace in a time of need. I want to thank You for the forgiveness you have shown me and I am humbled by all that I am and acknowledge before You now I need Your help in forgiving. I need You in every area of my life and I now know how important forgiveness is to You. I want to thank You for loving me enough to point this out to me. I now know that if I do not forgive others of their sins towards me then You cannot forgive me of my sins towards You and others. I have been judgmental of others and not of myself. I have been quick to point out the fault in my brother and sister and slow to look at myself. Lord Jesus, I want to forgive the way you forgive. I want to love the way you love. I need your help in forgiving.

In faith, and according to your commandments, I lay down all grudges, and malice I have had against anybody and everybody. I lay down all resentment and any unforgiveness I may have been holding on to in my heart. I release them to you forever in Jesus' name. I give You all the hurt that was caused me all my life and I ask You to come into my life and fill my heart with Your assurance of salvation and wash my conscience clean with Your love and grace.

I ask you to please forgive me now of every sin I have committed against You and others and from this day forward teach me and guide me in Your truth and Your ways.

Thank You for Your love and mercy, and Your gift of salvation and redemption through the blood of Jesus. Amen.

Chapter
12

Learning to Forgive

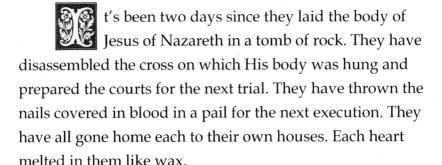 t's been two days since they laid the body of Jesus of Nazareth in a tomb of rock. They have disassembled the cross on which His body was hung and prepared the courts for the next trial. They have thrown the nails covered in blood in a pail for the next execution. They have all gone home each to their own houses. Each heart melted in them like wax.

Buried with Jesus was the hope of all mankind and the promise that God forgives man of their sins towards Him. His mother is in mourning for her son as she weeps all the day and night. She cannot be consoled as her memory of her brutalized son haunts her every thought. Her other sons embrace her with their arms around her tight, trying to console her but to no avail. When she is not looking, they themselves run away to cry alone in secret. Jesus' disciples are in hiding, fearing for their own lives. Their hearts are in a constant fear of uncertainty and dread. Am I next? What do we do now? Was He *really* the Messiah after all? What were His commands? Who is in charge now? Do I really want to do this? How can I get out of this city? What do we do? What do we do?

Each disciple has their own precious memory of their Lord, Matthew is remembering the warmth and peace from the smile the Master gave him as Jesus put his arms around him and thanked him for his hospitality at a time when Matthew was the most hated of all men. He loved him when no one else dared to. He looked up from the face of God and could see the stares of hatred written on each of the faces of the others in his house. Many are here with him now. "My, how things have changed since that day," he thought. "What has gone wrong? What can I do for you Lord, what do you want me to do?" *Nothing but silence.* "We are so frightened and you are locked away, why did they do that to you? Where are you now? Can you hear me? Can you see me? I'm sorry, I'm sorry." Matthew, remembering his precious friend, cries uncontrollably.

The hope that was birthed in the heart of man is now buried and dead, locked away behind a giant stone that seems so final. Early as the sun rises on the third day, the sun spreads its warm fingers of light across Israel's sand and stretches across the land to find the tomb of the Lord. Deep within its belly of earth a voice begins to break the silence as it calls out to the one lying still in the tomb. "Arise, My Son."

Just then the long spell of darkness is broken, as an Angel in white rolls the stone away and out of the earth rises the living, walking promise of God Himself! Light breaks forth and shatters the darkness once and for all as Jesus Christ victoriously walks out of his grave and into eternal life!

I wanted to give you the conclusion of the story from chapter one. It has a happy ending! I wouldn't have dreamed of telling you about the crucifixion and then leaving Jesus in the grave! Jesus died for our sins, but now He is alive forevermore! We started this book with a secret in chapter one and that was, the secret of forgiveness is **realizing the forgiveness that has been given to you**. I want to give you two more secrets before we end and the first one is this: while Jesus was on the cross He prayed for the people that were in fact executing Him. He cried out to His Father, **"Father, forgive them, for they do not know what they do"**(Luke 23:34). And that is the first secret. It's true, **we don't know what we are doing**. That prayer was not just for those that were executing Jesus, that was a prayer of forgiveness for all of mankind. **We really don't know what we are doing**. We think we do, we take the dominion over all given to us and the fact we are fearfully and wonderfully made and run with it. We live in our own little worlds and we think we know it all and have control of things but we are fooling ourselves. Man was given that power, but designed to walk hand and hand with God. However, man walks around oblivious to his true surrounding. Most of us walk carnally and not spiritually and leave a big wake of wounded around us. We don't realize every thing that someone has done to

us, we have done to someone else. There is no difference
between us and the soldier that drove the nails in our
Lord that day. We really don't know what we are doing!
Ever done something you were so sure of and when you
look back you say to yourself, "How could I have been so
stupid?" or "How could I have been so blind?" Well, we're
human, not God! We are made of the dirt of the ground.
We may have the spirit of God in us, but when we die our
spirit returns to the one who gave it and our body returns
to its natural form –dirt. We are the creation, not the
Creator. However, He remembers our frame and the fact
that we are made from the ground. I'm so glad, because I
put pressure on myself too much sometimes and when I
stumble He reminds me of that very fact. Mind you this
is not an excuse to hurt anyone or to excuse our sin. I'm
saying there are times when I really blew it and God led
me to **Psalm 103:14,** "For He knows our frame; he remembers
that we are dust." I would hear Jesus sing over me, "It's okay
son, I know you love Me."

You see, we are just human and we can't see past
the hand in front of our face. However, God can speak
the end from the beginning and that is why we should
never lean on our own understanding but in all our ways
acknowledge him (Proverbs 3:6)! You and I don't know
what is going to happen 3 seconds from now and God can
see through us and see our future. We really don't know
what we are doing. I am very weary of Mr. Preacher man
that is ranting and raving on my television set bragging

about this, preaching that and this and with such a fervent pitch. I sometimes catch flaws and wonder how long it will take him to realize he made a mistake in his theology. He will look back and go, "oh man, I blew it and I did it in front of millions." For instance, I saw one preacher point at the screen and preach sowing and reaping and multiplying. He said, "God multiplies our sowing a hundred fold and if you would give 10 dollars to His ministry right now God will give you a hundred! I thought to myself, "If he really believed that wouldn't he send me 10 dollars?"

It's Time to Forgive Yourself!

We really don't know what we are doing. Before we go to the second and final secret, I want you to really quiet down your heart for a moment and meditate on that truth. We are made from the dust and God knows this. We try to play God and be in charge so much we lose sight that God is in total control, not us. So if you have put too much pressure on yourself and have been trying to control everything, I want you to stop for a moment and put this book down on your chest and really meditate on what I am about to tell you. God loves you, He is in charge and no one can do anything about it. He is in charge, *not you* and He loves you and wants you to forgive yourself for all the mistakes you may hold against yourself.

He really does know you are human and made

from the dust of the ground. He knows you are trying to do your best. He loves you regardless of the mistakes and has factored in your human mistakes already when He died on the cross. Don't kick yourself over your failures or keep them locked away in some prison within you. Release them now to God and let He who is the lover of your soul and the Creator of all take over your worries. It's time to forgive yourself.

We Wrestle Not Against Flesh and Blood

For we do not wrestle against flesh and blood, but against principalities, against powers, against the rulers of darkness of this age, against spiritual hosts of wickedness in the heavenly places. Ephesians 6:12

This is a common scripture and one Christians can recite by heart; but how many of us truly know or understand what it is saying? Here lies our second secret in forgiveness. **We wrestle not against flesh and blood!** But against what? Against powers of darkness, spirits of wickedness. We must combat what is spiritual with the spiritual weapons God has given us for warfare. They are mighty through God, and we use them to pull down the strongholds that the enemy tries his best to fortify around us. **However the key is to see past the flesh *and face* of the person that is offending us and see what is really behind the situation.** To function properly and to mature as children of God, we must walk continually by the spirit, not by sight. For example, you may have found out by now that pastors are human. You see them do things or make decisions you absolutely know are wrong and you find it affecting the way you think about them. However, they are still called and chosen by God and we must look past their flesh and see the office they hold. The same goes for the President of the United Sates, our employer or our spouse; we must honor the office they hold.

Always remember we wrestle not against flesh and blood! Meaning, the father that is abusing you verbally or mentally is not really from the heart of your father but the spirit of disobedience behind your father. It's not your *father*; it's the spirit behind him. No one is born a homosexual; living a homosexual lifestyle is an action by choice. It's an action or behavior, not a person. There is a demonic spirit behind homosexuality. So the next time people are ready to judge anyone that confesses to be a homosexual, look past them, and see the spirit that is behind it. Anyone of us is prone to attack by our enemy and if we are not careful or mindful of this, we can say things that the enemy has whispered in our ears to hurt others. For a closer look at this Biblical principle, let's look at Job's wife in the book of Job in chapter 2.

Now keep in mind this is a test of Job's faith and integrity. Satan is betting that if he would take things away from Job he will turn his back on God. So Satan has thrown everything he could at Job, including taking his children and his health from him, and so we find Job sitting in a pile of ashes scraping his sores with a piece of broken pottery. His wife who is being manipulated by Satan himself comes up to Job and says,

"Are you still holding on to your integrity? Curse God and die!"

Now does that voice sound familiar? Was not the test in the first place to curse God, and to lose your integrity? It was not fully his wife who was speaking. She was being used like a puppet on a string. It was Satan, the spirit behind it. Listen to how Job responds to her in verse 10, "You are talking like a foolish woman. Shall we accept good from God, and not trouble?" He responds accordantly and with wisdom. We don't know what happened to Job's wife, the Bible doesn't say, we never hear from her again.

I'm sure Job could have looked at his wife naturally or in the flesh, and been confused or hurt by that outburst after all they have been through. But he didn't, he saw right past her and responded to the spirit that was behind it. We wrestle not against flesh and blood. But against what? Powers of darkness and wickedness.

Stop and think for a moment. Does God call for rape? Does the man that attacked the innocent jogger just naturally like raping women? It was the demonic spirit behind it. What about murder, lying, envy, adultery? The very fact that these things do not come from God testifies that they come from another source. A source that is hell bent on destruction. All our enemy does is steal, kill and destroy, but Jesus came so we could have life (John 10:10).

"We wrestle not against flesh and blood" is one of the most profound statements by the Apostle Paul in all his letters. It reminds us of the warfare we are under. We are always *under* this warfare. A mature son or daughter of Christ walks or lives by the spirit, not by sight, and a mature child of God understands our warfare is not carnal, it's spiritual. We walk in the spirit, see in the spirit, smell in the spirit and taste in the spirit. We must fully live in the spirit to maximize our walk or live fully with Jesus Christ, who Himself is now in an immortal human form and has released His Spirit (The Helper) unto us to help us, guide us, and walk with us till we should come to the fullness and knowledge of the truth.

All things were made by the spirit (He who is unseen) and all things are controlled by the spirit. What you see with your eyes is only temporary and is going away. What you see with your eyes is being controlled by God, (He who is unseen) and lives or exists through Him that made it. So we can say the things that aren't seen are more *real* than the things we can see. The things we can see are being controlled by the things we don't see. Nothing exists without God. So always see the way He sees. You are not being hurt or tormented by your father, mother, spouse, co-worker, or whoever has hurt you or wounded you. You are under the persecution through the carnal flesh of a fallen and sinful world, and by the devil who is mindful of man and in charge of those things of man.

Again, who does Paul say we wrestle against? Wickedness, powers of darkness, all those controlled by the spirit of him who is disobedient and opposite of God's ways and laws. We are persecuted by him who lives and works through the sons of disobedience, not mature sons of Christ.

Whether verbally, mentally or physically, our enemy is real and looks to destroy the life God gives us through Jesus Christ. We must know how the enemy works so we can know how to battle him. We must know his weapons and tricks so we can know how to process them. From this day forward when anyone says anything to try to wound you, I want you to remember to look past the person and remember we do not wrestle against flesh and blood. This must be learned over time and must be learned if we are to walk and grow in the Spirit.

A New Day A New Horizon

One day I found myself a steward of all the information you have read. I was thinking how did I get all this information on forgiveness? God put this book in my heart and I have poured myself morning by morning into the pages of this book so that you may know what God has revealed in me, and what I believe is an inspired book of God on the subject of something dear to His heart. Forgiveness.

I pray for you and trust that God has revealed some good things in your heart. I pray that you have been set free like a bird from its cage. Free to spread your wings again and soar high in the heavens among others that can sing the same beautiful song. A song of freedom, a song the angels can't sing, a song of redemption.

It's morning and as the darkness is losing its battle against the light of the day, the sun is dissolving the spell of night with rays that remind me of the goodness and promises of God. What will today bring? What will God have in store for me today? What ever comes my way, my Lord is with me, and as long as I know He is by my side it's okay if I stumble. It's enough to know He is there. I turn my face toward the sun and dream what new things and new horizons God has for me and His precious bride, His people. A day of hope, a day of redemption, a new day of forgiveness.

ABOUT THE AUTHOR

Jason Canady is an ordained minister that operates under an evangelistic anointing for restoring broken lives and pointing the way to a relationship with God. His main passion is to ignite the blaze of intimacy and zeal for the face of God. Jason preaches intimacy and a personal relationship with Jesus Christ through the power of the Holy Spirit.

Jason can be reached by writing to:

IVth Man Design
P.O. Box 9718
Fayetteville, N.C. 28311
jason@learntoforgive.org
Or you can visit us on the web at www.learntoforgive.org to learn more about Learning to Forgive, or to see other books offered by IVth Man Design. And for those who want to go deeper, you can read excerpts from his personal revelation knowledge or you can just email to say hello.

Do you have a testimony? Please contact us and encourage us with what God has done in your life through this book by emailing or writing us at the address above. We would love to hear from you.

About IVth Man Design.

This logo represents Integrity and Truth and you know when a book bears its mark you can trust the contents of the book. No publication will carry its mark unless the contents therein are intended for the edifying of the body of Christ. And the author's sole purpose is to lift up the name of Jesus Christ that He alone may be glorified.

IVth Man Design
P.O. Box 9718
Fayetteville, N.C. 28311
www.learntoforgive.org

Order a personalized copy of

Learning To Forgive

$10.00 Cover price
plus $2.00 shipping charge per book

QTY of Book(s) _____

Please send check or money order
and make payable to:

IVth Man Design
PO Box 9718
Fayetteville, NC 28311

Allow 2 to 4 weeks for delivery.

Name: _____

Address: _____

_____

City: _____

State: _____ Zip: _____

❏ Yes I would like my book personally signed by the author.

Personalized information:

_____

_____

Also look for other great titles and other information at our website at:

www.learntoforgive.org